ARE YOU COMPUTER LITERATE?

ARE YOU COMPUTER LITERATE?

Karen Billings
and
David Moursund

dilithium Press
Beaverton, Oregon

© Copyright, Karen Billings and David Moursund, 1979

10 9 8 7 6

All rights reserved. No part of this book may be reproduced in any form or by any means without permission in writing from the publisher, with the following two exceptions: any material may be copied or transcribed for the non-profit use of the purchaser; and material (not to exceed 300 words and one figure) may be quoted in published reviews of this book.

ISBN: 0-918398-29-0
Library of Congress catalog card number: 79-56396

Printed in the United States of America.

dilithium Press
P.O. Box 606
Beaverton, OR 97075

PREFACE

Computers are helping to change business, education and government. They are changing what we need to learn, and how we learn it. They are creating new jobs and wiping out or changing old ones.

For many years the leaders in computer science and mathematics education have stated that everyone should be learning something about computers. They recommend that people learn the capabilities, limitations, applications, and implications of computers. They suggest that all people be given the opportunity to gain substantial "hands-on" experience with computers. These computer experts recommend that computer literacy instruction be incorporated into all secondary schools.

This book is designed to help people become more computer literate. It does not assume any previous experience with computers, nor does it require that any particular computer equipment be available. The book can be used in conjunction with introductory instruction in computer programming, or it can be used for a computer literacy unit offered in a social studies, science, mathematics, or business education course.

The format of the book is particularly suited to self instruction. Quizzes at the beginning of Chapters 2 through 8, and a Final Exam, allow the reader to chart his or her progress. It is recommended that you take the chapter quizzes twice—before and after reading each chapter.

Each chapter contains a number of activities, suggested readings, and sources of information. Some activities are based upon ideas covered in the chapter, while others contain related additional information. It is important that you read and think about the activities, even if you do not complete all of them.

CONTENTS

HELLO — 1
   Do you know a lot about computers — 1
   What you already know — 3
   Why you need to know more — 6

WHAT IS A COMPUTER? — 11
   What is a computer? — 12
   Pocket calculators — 12
   Computers — 14

WHY DO COMPUTERS EXIST? — 27
   Why do computers exist? — 28
   Early history — 28
   Written aids — 29
   Mechanical calculators — 30
   The Jacquard loom — 30
   The analytical engine — 31
   The U.S. census of 1890 — 32
   Relay computers — 33
   The electronic digital computer — 34
   Modern computers — 35

DATA ENTRY AND COMPUTER PROGRAMMING — 39
   Computer limitations — 40
   Data — 40
   Computer programming — 43
   Summary — 47

SMART MACHINES 55
   Smart machines 56
   Process control 56
   Assembly line robots 58
   Robot game number one 59
   Robot game number two 62
   Summary 63

HOW COMPUTERS ARE BEING USED 69
   How computers are being used 69
   Modeling 70
   Mathematical modeling 71
   Computer simulation 72
   Information retrieval 73
   Data processing 77
   Conclusion 79

HOW COMPUTERS AFFECT PEOPLE 91
   Computers affect people 92
   Goods and services 92
   Jobs 94
   Education 96
   Big brother is watching you 98
   Computer careers 100
   Conclusions 101

WHAT ELSE IS THERE TO KNOW?
   Computer literacy 112
   Using computers 113
   Computer programming 116
   Computer science 118
   What should you do? 121

ADDITIONAL RESOURCES 127
   Resource books 127
   Computer films 128
   Information, please 130
   Computers and music 131

COMPUTER LITERACY EXAM 133

GLOSSARY 141

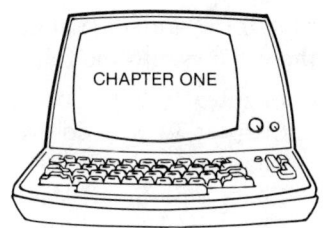

HELLO

CHAPTER ONE

DO YOU KNOW A LOT ABOUT COMPUTERS?

That's hard to answer with a simple "yes" or "no." You do know many things about computers, but much of what you think you know you probably learned from television. You may think computers are like people in many ways, only smarter. Maybe you believe that computers are sinister and trying to take over the world. These are the ways in which computers are portrayed in many movies and television programs, but it isn't the way there are in the real world!

This book will help you learn more about computers (and robots, calculators, and related things). It won't teach you all there is to know about computers, but it will get you headed in the right direction.

This first chapter discusses some of the things you may already know about computers. As you read it you will probably see that there are some things you don't know. We have divided these things into the following major topics:

Chapter 2: What is a Computer?
Chapter 3: Why do Computers Exist?
Chapter 4: Data-Entry and Computer Programming
Chapter 5: Smart Machines
Chapter 6: How Computers are Being Used
Chapter 7: How Computers Affect People
Chapter 8: What Else is there to Know?

Each of these chapters begins with a quiz. As you start each topic, try testing yourself to see how much you already know about it. If you get *all* of the questions right on one of the quizzes, it shows you are familiar with that aspect of computers. But even then, you will learn some interesting new things by reading that chapter.

At the end of each chapter there are some activities for you to try. These give you a chance to test yourself on the material just presented, or to extend your knowledge.

There is a Computer Literacy Exam at the end of this book. If you read the book carefully, you should be able to do very well on the final exam. Right now we will give you a chance to learn the answer to the first question on that exam.

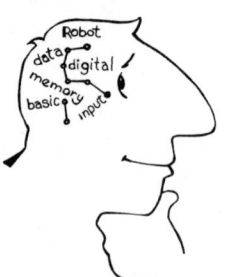

Retrieve from your primary storage

Now its your turn!

1. What is computer literacy? Is it:
   a. The ability to write computer programs?
   b. Knowing what a computer can and cannot do, how computers are used, and how they may change our lives?
   c. Knowing computer-related vocabulary, so you can read, write, and talk about computers?
   d. Understanding how to build a computer?

The whole purpose of this book is to help you become more computer literate. The best answer to the question is "b." But

Hello 3

as you read this book you will also learn some computer vocabulary which will make you better at reading and talking about computers.

WHAT YOU ALREADY KNOW

The first general purpose electronic digital computer began operation in December, 1945. Thus, more than half of the people in the United States today were born after the birth of the first computer. People learn about computers from television, movies, books, magazines, newspapers, electronic games, and friends. All of these give out information about computers—some of it correct, and some of it incorrect.

A little thinking will help you realize that you do know a great deal about computers. For example, an electronic pocket calculator might be thought of as a limited-purpose computer, having many characteristics of a full scale computer. It can be

used to input and store numbers, carry out arithmetic on those numbers, and output answers. If you know something about calculators (Do you own one? Have you ever used one?) then you know something about computers.

Have you ever looked at or filled out an income tax return? This information is input to a computer, which checks it for errors and attempts to detect cases of cheating. The federal

government receives about 100 million tax returns each year. Checking all of these income tax returns is a big job, even for a computer.

You probably use a telephone almost every day. The telephone system is very computerized. If you make a mistake in dialing, a computerized voice may tell you so. A computer routes calls to their proper destinations and gathers billing information. Computers prepare the monthly bills. Thus, when you use a telephone, you are making use of a computer. Some computers are very easy to use!

Have you ever watched the election night voting returns on television? Computers are used to count ballots, and to make projections on probable winners. These projections are possible because computers analyze large amounts of data quickly and accurately.

Have you ever flown in a commercial airplane? Computers are essential tools of the air traffic controllers, who use them to help insure that planes don't crash into each other. Computers are also used inside the plane to keep track of fuel consumption and the plane's position. A computerized device, the autopilot, can even fly the plane.

Do you read a newspaper? Many newspaper publishers use computers to do their typesetting. Computers have taken over some tasks that used to be done by highly skilled workers. For example, computers can hyphenate words to make lines the right length for a newspaper column.

Did you know that some new cars contain built-in computers? The computer helps improve gas mileage by controlling the mixture of gasoline and air in the carburetor. Computers are also used in automobile manufacturing. Computerized robots are beginning to take over some of the assembly line jobs. They can weld parts together, screw nuts onto bolts, etc. It is claimed that they are cheaper and more reliable than people.

Have you ever played Pong or other electronic video games? The games themselves are fairly low cost, and many of them

contain their own built in computers. These computers are rapidly becoming an important form of entertainment.

Have you been in a hospital in the last few years? Your blood was probably typed and analyzed by a computerized testing device. Maybe your brain waves or heart beat were analyzed by a computer, or perhaps a computerized X-ray machine was used to do a full body X-ray.

Have you seen a letter written by a computer? Companies mail out millions of these letters each year, trying to get people to subscribe to their magazine or buy their products. The letters

mention your name and maybe your neighbor's name. The idea is to fool you into believing they have written and typed a special letter just for you!

Do you listen to weather forecasts on radio or television? These reports are prepared by computers. In recent years, long range weather forecasts have become much more accurate due to increases in the speed and capacity of computers. This is especially important to farmers who must decide what crops to plant and when to plant them.

Have you seen bills printed by a computer? All large companies use computers for bookkeeping and processing charge card bills. Many department stores keep track of their inventory using the same machines. Computers are an essential part of many businesses.

Are you a student, or have you been a student in the past few years? Computers are now quite commonly used in schools.

Many schools use them for registration, for keeping track of attendance, and for printing report cards. Computers are also used to do the payroll computations for the school district.

Do you have a social security card or a driver's license? If so, your name and number is recorded somewhere. Do you know where? Do you know people who receive veteran's benefits, social security payments, medicare, welfare payments, or unemployment payments? How do you think all of this information is handled? Have you seen a policeman stop a speeding car, and then radio in the license number? What is done with this information? What becomes of the information collected by local and state police, and the FBI? The answer to these and many other questions is the same: the computer is used to store and analyze the data.

WHY YOU NEED TO KNOW MORE

Computers create questions that you will have to answer, and problems that you will have to help solve. Let's look at a simple example. One outgrowth of computer technology is the pocket calculator. It can add, subtract, multiply, and divide. Calculators are so cheap that almost everybody can afford one, and schools could provide them to all students. Should they? How should calculators affect the teaching of elementary school mathematics? Is it really important to learn to do long division using pencil and paper?

Computers can solve many different kinds of problems. Some of these are problems that people study in elementary or secondary school. If a computer can solve a problem, how important is it for students to learn how to solve it by hand? We can ask the same question about other machines, such as a bulldozer. One does not try to compete with a bulldozer in moving large amounts of dirt, but there are many tasks that are better done with a hand shovel.

You know that computers are important in automation. They may help to destroy some old jobs, but they create some new ones. What career do you seek? How will computers affect this career? Perhaps it will be wiped out by computers in five or ten years. Do you know enough about computers to make an intelligent career decision?

In the United States the largest user of computers is the federal government (counting the military). One thing governments try to do is to collect information in order to make decisions. The federal government keeps detailed information on taxpayers, businesses, people holding social security cards, people receiving social security and medicare payments, people with FBI records, people who have been in the military, etc. The government also requires businesses to keep detailed records. For example, every check processed by a bank is microfilmed by the bank.

What information *should* the government collect about people? Who should have access to this information? How should the information be used? These are very difficult questions that must be answered by voters and lawmakers.

Computers make decisions or help make decisions affecting all of us. Sometimes we are not happy with the results. For example, a highway patrolman is parked beside the freeway, watching cars go by, when a speeding car is detected. The patrolman notes the license number and radios it in. Meanwhile the chase is on. Just as the speeding car is stopping the radio reports back that the car is stolen. The patrolman gets out of the patrol car; the driver of the speeding car gets out of his car and reaches into his pocket. The patrolman thinks he is reaching for a gun, draws his revolver, and shoots!

Actually, the car was reported stolen two weeks ago, and was recovered the next day. The information that it was recovered was not entered into the computer information system. The driver of the speeding car was the owner. He was reaching into his pocket to take out his driver's license. Now he is dead! Are computers responsible?

As computers become cheaper they will be used more widely. Their impact upon your life will increase. This can be frightening, but knowledge will help you to cope. That is why you need to know more about computers.

THINK ABOUT COMPUTERS

MICROCOMPUTERS AT HOME

Very small, quite cheap computers, called microcomputers, are now built into many devices found in the home. Examples are toys, automobiles, microwave ovens, burglar alarm systems and TV video games. In fact, a complete general purpose microcomputer system now costs about as much as a color television set. They are becoming a common household item.

Do you know someone with a new car? Ask the owner if there is a microcomputer in it and if so, what it does for the car.

Do you know anyone with a TV video game, a hand-held calculator-like toy, or a complete computer? If so, how long have they had it? Have the prices come down on these devices in the past few years?

Hello

WHAT COMPUTERS CAN AND CAN'T DO

Make a list of at least five different things that you think computers *can* do, but which people cannot do.

example: work efficiently for 100 hours without stopping

What are some things that computers *cannot* do, but which people can do.

example: express feelings

TRAFFIC LIGHTS

Many traffic lights now are controlled by computers. Find out if some of the traffic lights in your town or city are controlled by a computer. Do you think it is possible for a computer to make a traffic light show green in all directions. Suppose that a computer did this, and a serious accident resulted. Who would be to blame?

COMPUTERS IN YOUR LIFE

Are computers discussed at school?

Write in the chart below three courses you are taking now (or took recently enough to remember well). Select them from three different subject fields (like music, language arts, mathematics, science and others). Then think about the effect that computers have had on the field, then on the course itself. (If you have children in school, you might fill this out for some courses they are taking.)

Course Subject	Use of Computers in that field	Computers mentioned by: teacher? text? other?

Will you use a computer in your career? Write down several careers in which you are interested, then the effect that computers have had or may have on each of them. (If you are employed, include your current career.)

Career Field	Effect of computers or automation on it

Would you vote for a computer? Computers help run the country now. Do you think a computer could be a good president of the U.S.? Give some arguments for and against it.

Yes, because...	No, because...

CHAPTER TWO

WHAT IS A COMPUTER?

How much do you already know about computers? Test yourself by answering true or false to these questions. The correct answers are given in the back of the book.

T F (1) Computers are very smart. They can answer almost any question.
T F (2) Computers can work with words as well as with numbers.
T F (3) A calculator is an example of an electronic digital computer.
T F (4) A computer can easily do millions of calculations in an hour.
T F (5) A computer's memory is very much like a human's memory.
T F (6) Computers can cost several million dollars, or as little as a few hundred dollars.
T F (7) The price of computers has been rapidly increasing in the past few years.
T F (8) Magnetic tape can be used as a computer memory device.
T F (9) A computer program is a television program about computers.
T F (10) A large computer may have a memory large enough to store an entire encyclopedia of information.

WHAT IS A COMPUTER?

The word computer has many definitions. Sometimes a very smart person is called a computer. Sometimes a measuring device such as a speedometer or a thermometer is called a computer. Sometimes a pocket calculator is called a computer.

But as far as this book is concerned, none of these are computers. Here the word computer refers to a special kind of machine—an *electronic digital computer*. The word electronic suggests that the machine uses electricity and operates very fast. The word digital suggests that the machine works with the digits 0, 1, 2, . . . 9. Actually an electronic digital computer also works with the alphabet, and with punctuation marks and other special characters. Computers are not limited to working with numbers only, and most applications do not involve solving math problems.

POCKET CALCULATORS

The battery-powered pocket calculator is not a computer, but it does have many computer-like features. Calculators are enough like computers so that we can learn a lot about computers by studying calculators. We will begin by listing some of the things you probably already know about calculators. Then we will show how computers are like calculators, and how they are different from calculators.

Suppose you wanted to use a simple calculator to divide 827.39 by 29.8. You would proceed as follows:

1. Turn on the calculator.
2. Depress the keys 827.39 ÷ 29.8 =
3. Read the answer 27.764765 displayed by the calculator.

What is a Computer?

What could be easier? Even if you had never used a calculator before, you could learn to divide on it in just a few seconds.

The calculator is a marvelous invention. It is cheap, easy to use, and easy to learn how to use. More important, it performs difficult tasks quickly, tasks such as multiplication and division of big numbers. Calculators help people solve problems that they would normally find hard to do by hand.

It is easy to understand what a calculator is and what it can do. By itself, a calculator can't do anything. It is just a machine that sits there until it is turned on and "told" what to do. The person using a calculator must provide it with the data to be processed (for example, the two numbers to be divided) and the operation to be performed (add, subtract, multiply, or divide). The person must also push the = (equals) key, telling the calculator to carry out the indicated operation. Only then can the calculator carry out a computation and display the answer. Let's summarize what a calculator can do. A calculator can:

1. Accept and remember data (numbers) keyed in using its keyboard.
2. Accept and remember an instruction (what operation to use) keyed in using its keyboard.
3. When instructed to do so, automatically carry out the operation on the data.
4. Output the answer (show it on its printer or lighted display).

As you can see, a calculator isn't a very smart machine. It can do things like long division very well, but that is just a mechanical, non-thinking process. The person using the calculator must do whatever thinking is needed in solving a problem.

COMPUTERS

While most calculators can only work with numbers, computers can work with letters and punctuation marks (and hence, words, sentences, etc.) as well as with numbers. Thus computers can do everything calculators can do and much, much more.

In the last section we made a list of the four general types of things a calculator can do. Now we will make a similar list for computers.

1. **Data:** Anything that can be typed on a typewriter can be input to a computer. Indeed, a special kind of electric typewriter, called a keyboard terminal, is often hooked directly to a computer. Thus the data to be processed by a computer can consist of both words and numbers. It can include people's names and addresses, school records, criminal records, and even complete books.

2. **Instructions:** A simple calculator has one key for each instruction that it "understands" how to do. The very simplest calculator has only four of these keys—it understands only four different instructions. A more expensive calculator may have several dozen instruction keys. Such a calculator can carry out any one of several dozen different instructions.

The typical computer understands 100 to 200 different instructions. More important, it can remember a list or sequence of instructions designed by a person to solve some problem. This list of instructions is called a *computer program*. The person who designs and writes the list of instructions is called a *computer programmer*.

```
1∅  DIM M$ (12), N(12)
2∅  FOR I=1 TO 12
3∅  READ M$ (I), N(I)
4∅  NEXT I
5∅  FOR I=∅ TO 6
6∅
```

What is a Computer?

A computer program can be hundreds or even many thousands of instructions in length. It is a very detailed set of directions telling the machine exactly what to do in order to solve a particular type of problem. A computer is merely an electronic device that can follow these instructions. The computer programmer must do all of the thinking required to figure out how to solve the problem.

3. **Automatic:** After data and instructions are made available to a computer, it can automatically carry out the instructions. Carrying out the instructions is called *executing* a program. Computers can do this kind of work very quickly. A fast modern computer can execute millions of instructions in one second!

You are familiar with other automatic machines, such as an automatic clothes washer, or a dishwasher. These machines automatically carry out an appropriate sequence of wash, rinse, and spin dry or dry cycles. These machines have several different "programs" that they can follow. For example, you may be able to direct a washing machine to use cold, warm, or hot water; to wash a small, medium, or large load; and to wash it for the number of minutes you specify. A computer differs from these machines in that it can accept a very complicated program and then carry out the steps in the program very rapidly.

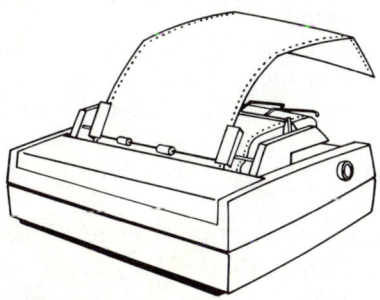

4. **Output:** A computer can output the answers it produces. Often it uses a keyboard terminal for output. But for some problems a keyboard terminal is too slow. For example, suppose a computer was being used to type address labels for every student in a large school district. This could take hundreds of hours on a keyboard terminal. To obtain faster output, many computers have an output device called a line printer. It prints an entire line at one time, and can print several hundred times as fast as a fast typist.

Computer Limitations

What a computer can do depends upon just four things:

1. Can a program be written that gives exact instructions on what needs to be done?
2. Can the necessary data be obtained and made available to the computer?
3. Is the storage capacity of the computer big enough to hold the program and data?
4. Is the computer fast enough to execute the program in a reasonable period of time?

Chapter 4 is concerned with the first two points. The rest of this chapter is used to discuss the last two points.

Computer Speed

One of the most impressive features of a computer is its speed. Computers are very fast. How long would it take you to do the division 827.39 ÷ 29.8 using pencil and paper? Can you do it in one minute? In that length of time a computer could do millions of division problems! *A fast modern computer can do more arithmetic in one minute than a person using a pencil and paper could do in a lifetime*! And the computer can do this without making any mistakes.

Generally speaking the more expensive a computer is, the faster it is. But even an inexpensive computer is very fast. A computer costing just a few hundred dollars can do half a million arithmetic computations in one minute. The most expensive computers, costing a few million dollars, are about a thousand times this fast.

It is difficult to understand the meaning of the big numbers used to describe a computer's speed. Consider the speeds of a person walking, a person driving a car, and a person flying in an airplane. Suppose each were trying to go clear across the United States—a distance of about 3,000 miles (4827 Km). The person walking would take many months. This is not something one does just to visit a relative. The person driving might make it in a week. The person flying could make in in less than half a day. A business trip that takes one across the country and back is a fairly common thing for some people. But an airplane is only 100 to 200 times as fast as a walking person. Computers can do arithmetic more than a million times as fast as a person using a

What is a Computer?

pencil and paper! The computer thus makes it possible to solve many problems that would be completely impossible to do by hand. Most modern advances in science, engineering, and medicine are made possible by the availability of high speed computers.

Computer Memory

A computer memory is in no sense like a human memory. A much better comparison is that a computer memory is like a tape recorder. Storing data in a computer memory is much like recording it on magnetic tape. The data can be erased when it is no longer needed, or it can be saved for many years.

Most computer systems have at least two kinds of memory devices. One kind, called *primary memory*, functions very fast but is small in total capacity. The other, called *secondary memory*, doesn't function as fast, but can have a very large capacity.

A comparison with humans gives insight into primary and secondary storage. You can memorize small amounts of data that you need to use quite often. Thus you memorize your telephone number, name, and address, some addition and multiplication facts, and how to spell many different words. Then

you can retrieve all of this data very rapidly. This is like primary storage.

Secondary storage is like use of reference books. The telephone book stores the name, address, and telephone number of thousands of people. It takes a while to look up data on a particular person, but few people would be able to memorize an entire telephone directory.

The primary memory of a computer must be able to function as fast as the machine's computational speed. One very common type of primary memory is called *core* memory, and is made from donut-shaped cores of electromagnetic material which are about 1 to 2 mm in diameter. Another type is made from transistors and other electronic components, and is called *solid-state* memory. Both types have decreased in price in recent years, and solid-state memory is now cheaper than core memory. Still, primary memory is quite expensive for a given amount of storage, as compared to secondary memory. Thus, the primary memory of most computer systems has a much smaller storage capacity than the secondary memory.

The "size" of a computer memory is a statement of how many characters of data (how many digits, letters and punctuation marks) it can contain. An inexpensive computer (one costing under $1,000) will generally have a primary memory that can store a few thousand characters. This is like storing a couple of pages of typed material. A very expensive computer will have a primary memory that can store a few million characters. A million characters is about the length of a good-sized book. The book you are now reading is only about one-fifth that long.

There are many forms of secondary memory. Magnetic tape and related devices are common. Inexpensive computers often use an ordinary cassette tape recorder as a secondary storage device. The magnetic material used to make magnetic tape can also be used to coat a circular platter called a magnetic *disk*. Disks are rotated much like a phonograph record, only at a much higher speed. A read/write head can be rapidly moved to any spot on the disk to write information on it or read data from it. Data on any spot on the disk can be reached in a fraction of a second.

Often a number of magnetic disks are banded together with air space in between to allow movement of read/write heads.

This is called a *disk pack*. A modern disk pack sells for about $500, and can store 600 million characters of data. That is roughly the same as storing 600 full length books in a space about a foot in diameter and half a foot high.

Of course the disk pack itself is not the only expense in using disks for secondary memory. A disk drive mechanism is needed to spin the disk pack rapidly. Very precise machinery is needed to position the read/write heads. A disk drive can cost many thousands of dollars, but compared to the cost of primary memory it is still a very cheap way to store a large amount of data.

Two new types of secondary memory devices began to be sold in 1977. These are *charge-coupled devices* and *magnetic bubble* memory. When these first began to be sold they were considerably more expensive than disk per character of storage. But they are still less expensive than primary memory. They have no moving parts, which makes them very reliable and faster than disk memory. As these devices are mass produced they will decrease in price, and will replace disk memory in many applications.

Summary

To sum up, computers are very fast and have very large storage capacity. There are some problems that exceed the speed and storage capacity of computers, but most problems are not this big. Also, each year, progress enables us to make faster computers and larger and cheaper memory devices. If you have a problem that is too big for today's computers, all you have to do is wait a few years. About 5 to 10 years from now you will be able to buy a computer that is 10 times as fast, and has 10 times as much memory—at the same cost as today's machine. Of course, this sort of progress cannot continue forever, but it has been continuing for many years and is likely to continue for at least 5 or 10 more years.

TO THINK ABOUT

Is there a calculator in your home?
If so, who uses it in the family? For what reasons?
Are all the keys on the calculator used?
Do you think you could become too dependent on a calculator?
Give reasons for and against being able to use it whenever you wanted to.

IF YOU ARE INTERESTED...

Here are some calculator books you may enjoy:

Take a Chance with Your Calculator, Lennart Rade, dilithium Press, Portland, OR, 1977
Games, Tricks, and Puzzles for a Hand Calculator, Wallace Judd, dilithium Press, Portland, OR, 1974
Games with the Pocket Calculator, Thiagarajan/Stolovitch, dilithium Press, Portland, OR, 1976
Countdown, Eisburg/Hyde, dilithium Press, Portland, OR, 1979

What is a Computer?

WHAT GETS THE COMPUTER CHECK-UP?

Shade the box under the most appropriate response.

Turn your paper around sideways to find out the name of a company that uses computers to help design and build its cars— as well as to diagnose engine problems for the owners.

	Both	4-Function Calculator	Computer	Neither
1. It is used as an aid to problem solving.	▓			
2. Most of its uses are solving math-type problems.				
3. It can process words as well as numbers.				
4. It keeps getting more and more expensive.				
5. It can use a keyboard terminal for input and output.				
6. It can solve any problem imaginable.				
7. It uses magnetic tape and disk for secondary storage.				
8. It has a key for each "instruction" it understands.				
9. It is a digital computing device.				
10. It carries out computations and outputs an answer.				
11. It can be purchased for $10 or less.				
12. It can use an output device called a line printer.				
13. It can operate without being told what to do.				
14. It can cost a few hundred to a few million dollars.				
15. It is usually portable and battery powered.				
16. It contains electronic circuitry.				

LET'S CALCULATE

If you have a hand calculator you can use, try these activities.

The Age-Old Problem

Input the number of your birth month (Jan = 1, Feb = 2 ...) and multiply it by 100 on your calculator.
Add the day of the month in which you were born.
Then multiply by 2 and add 9.
Multiply by 5 and add 8.
Multiply by 10 and subtract 422.
Add your age and subtract 108.

The result is a 5 or 6 digit number. Three sets of numbers should be recognizable:

First set = the month you were born
Second set = the date you were born
Third set (on right) = your age

Can you explan why the calculator was able to display the right numbers?

Is It Perfect?

Take a 3-digit number like 200. Reverse it (002) and then multiply the two numbers.

$$200 \times 002$$

The result is 400 or a perfect square (20 × 20 = 400). Find all such 3-digit numbers. Keep a record of the ones you find.

What Did the Red Baron Put in Snoopy's House?

Multiply one hundred one by the square of three.
Add fifty.
Multiply by each of the counting numbers *between* six and nine.
Turn the calculator upside down. Read the answer on the display.

CHAPTER THREE

WHY DO COMPUTERS EXIST?

How much do you know about the history of computers? Test yourself by answering true or false to these questions. The correct answers are given in the back of the book.

T F (1) One of the first aids to computation, the abacus, was invented nearly a thousand years ago.
T F (2) The first 4-function mechanical calculators were built during the 1600s.
T F (3) Punched cards were used in the Jacquard loom to help automate the weaving of cloth during the early 1800s.
T F (4) Punched cards were used by Herman Hollerith to process the United States census of 1776.
T F (5) Charles Babbage is noted primarily for building the first hand held electronic calculator.
T F (6) The telephone, automobile, radio and television were all invented before the electronic digital computer.
T F (7) The first electronic digital computers did not contain transistors or core memory.
T F (8) Early electronic digital computers broke down quite often, due to burnt out vacuum tubes.
T F (9) IBM is now the world's largest computer company.
T F (10) In the computer field, a "chip" is a scratch or dent that seriously damages a piece of computing machinery.

WHY DO COMPUTERS EXIST?

Our society makes use of many instruments and machines, such as the telephone, automobile, airplane, radio, and television. Each was designed to solve some problem or overcome some obstacle. So it is with computers. A computer is a general purpose aid to problem solving in many different fields. By studying the history of computers we can see what types of problems the first computers were designed to solve. We can also see how changes in technology have led to the modern, high speed, general purpose computer.

EARLY HISTORY

More than 10,000 years ago people were interested in counting things and keeping numerical records. They used notches on

a stick, scratches on a rock, and charcoal marks on the wall of a cave. These marks could be used to record the passage of days, or to keep track of the size of one's flock.

But counting and arithmetic are not easy to learn, and many people had trouble with them. The *abacus* was invented about 5,000 years ago to help people solve counting and simple arithmetic problems. This machine was so successful that some

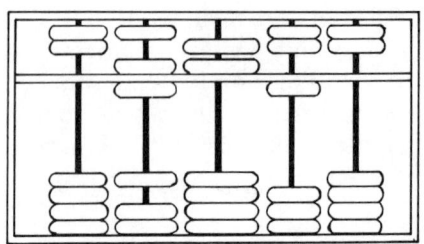

people still use it today. A person who is highly skilled with an abacus can do many arithmetic problems as fast as a person using a calculator, but it takes considerable training and experience to develop this level of skill.

Even with the invention of the abacus, counting and arithmetic continued to be difficult problems for most people. Two different types of progress have occurred towards overcoming these problems. One is the invention of better machines, and that is what most of this chapter is about. The other is vocabulary and written language. We will discuss this briefly in the next section.

WRITTEN AIDS

Language is an important aid to counting and computation. You probably know about one of the early number systems. These are Roman numerals.

I II III IV V VI VII VIII IX X XI XII

It is not too hard to learn to use Roman numerals for simple counting. They are harder if one wants to write down a large number. For example, how would you like to have to learn that the Declaration of Independence was signed in MDMCCLXXVI?

The Mayans used a system of dots representing ones, and bars representing fives. Although the Romans and Mayans did not

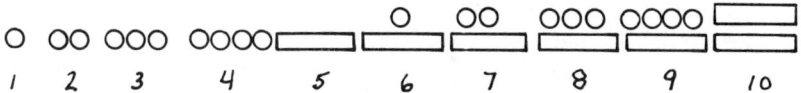

know of each other's existence, they both developed a number system based upon ones and fives. Can you think of good reasons why this happened?

The number system we now use, called the Hindu-Arabic numeral system, was developed more than 1,500 years ago. It is easier than Roman numerals, especially if one wants to deal with big numbers. It is also much better suited to learning to do arithmetic. You may think that carrying out a division such as 2544 divided by 53 is difficult. But imagine trying to learn how to solve problems such as MMDXLIV divided by LIII. It is no wonder that in ancient times people who were good at arithmetic were often considered to be wizards!

MECHANICAL CALCULATORS

In grade school you were taught how to divide two numbers by a process called long division. You also learned processes for addition, subtraction and multiplication. The processes you learned are not new; all of them were invented before the year 1600. These basic processes are not easy to learn, and most people have to study and practice for a long time in order to learn them. Thus it is not surprising to learn that in Europe in the 1600's, most people could not do "hard" problems such as multiplication and division. These were topics that people studied in certain specialized colleges!

To solve this problem people began to build machines which could do arithmetic. Wilhelm Schickard developed a mechanical calculator in 1623. It could add, subtract, multiply, and divide. It was the first machine that could perform these four functions. Later other people re-invented the calculator. Blaise Pascal is well known for the calculator he built in 1642, as well as for his work in mathematics.

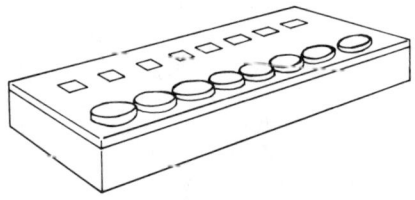

But the early mechanical calculators were expensive and not very reliable, and nearly 200 years passed before calculators began to be commonly available. Even then, they were used mainly by businesses and scientists. School children and most adults did not have access to calculators.

THE JACQUARD LOOM

A very important part of the history of computers had nothing to do with numbers or mathematics. Joseph-Marie Jacquard was a Frenchman interested in building a better machine for weaving cloth. In 1801 he introduced the idea of using punched cards to control the raising and lowering of threads on a loom. Small metal rods would press against a card. If a hole was found, the rod would move down, moving the threads attached to it. With a Jacquard loom, one person could now do the work that previously required two people.

Why Do Computers Exist?

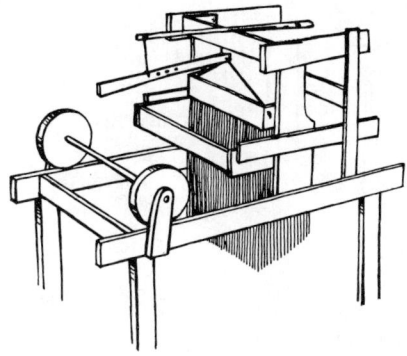

Jacquard's invention was a very important idea. The set of directions telling which threads to raise or lower could be coded as holes in cards. A machine could "read" these punched cards, and automatically follow the directions.

The Jacquard loom was a computer-like machine. It was very successful, and by 1812, about 11,000 of them were being used in France. Some are still in use today. They decreased the cost of woven materials, but put many weavers out of work.

THE ANALYTICAL ENGINE

There are many math-type problems that occur over and over again. It is possible to solve these problems and put the answers in a book, allowing people to look them up instead of doing the work of figuring them out. Such a book is called a book of math *tables*. In the 1800s and before that people spent a lot of time developing navigational tables, interest tables, artillery firing tables, eclipse prediction tables, etc.

Thus it was not too surprising that someone decided to try to combine the ideas of Jacquard with those of the mechanical calculator. The goal was to make a mechanical calculator that could automatically carry out a sequence of mathematical instructions. This machine could be instructed to produce a math table contining solutions to certain standard problems.

Charles Babbage, an Englishman, developed the ideas for such a machine in 1835. He called the machine an analytical engine. The machine would use punched cards to contain a program — the instructions that the calculator was to carry out. Unfortunately, the machine proved to be too hard and too expensive to build. Even though Babbage worked on it for many years, he

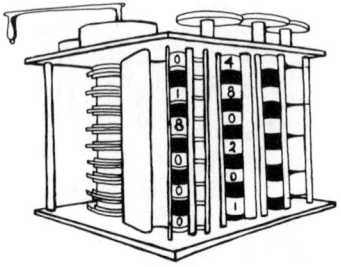

was not able to complete a working model. However, he and another mathematician named Lady Lovelace, worked together to discover many of the ideas of modern computers. Lady Lovelace, daughter of the well known poet, Lord Byron, is now considered to be the world's first computer programmer.

THE U.S. CENSUS OF 1890

Every 10 years the United States government counts all of its people, and asks them some questions about their income, housing, etc. This is called taking a census.

After the census data is gathered, it is processed to answer questions such as "What percentage of families own the house they live in?" and "How many families have 5 or more children?" The census data of 1880 took *7 years* to process.

Thus it was clear that a serious problem was going to occur with the 1890 census. The population had increased rapidly and the government wanted to ask more questions. It was going to take more than 10 years to process all of the data unless a new method could be developed. That was serious, because by then the 1900 census data would be waiting to be processed.

Herman Hollerith found a solution. He suggested that the data be recorded in the form of holes punched in cards. He built machines that could automatically sort and count the cards. Using his machines the 1890 census data was processed in just *3 years*. That is truly amazing, since this involved the punching and processing of 63 million data cards.

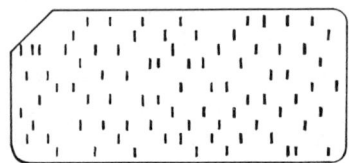

Why Do Computers Exist?

Herman Hollerith started a company to produce the punch card equipment he invented. Later, his company joined with another company to form International Business Machines (IBM). IBM produced card punches, card sorters, card counters, card duplicators, etc. All of this equipment was useful to businesses, so IBM grew into a large company. This occurred a long time before the first electronic digital computer was built.

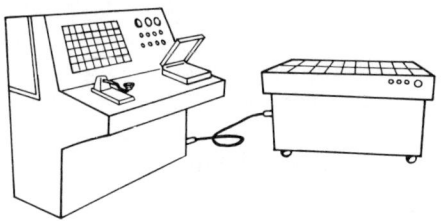

RELAY COMPUTERS

Early mechanical calculators used a hand crank for their power source. After electricity became available, some calculators were powered by electric motors. These electromechanical calculators were developed before 1900, and they were faster and easier to use than their simple mechanical predecessors.

In the late 1930s people again began to work on the idea of building an automated calculator. They duplicated much of the thinking of Charles Babbage, but the technology available to them was much improved. They decided to make use of a type of switching device used in telephone circuitry called an electrical *relay*. A relay can be opened and closed very rapidly, using electrical current. This is like turning a switch off and on.

IBM helped sponsor the building of one of the early "relay" computers. It was built at Harvard University and completed in 1944. This machine was called the Mark I. It took about six seconds to do a multiplication and twelve seconds to do a division. Its speed for single computations was about that of an electromechanical calculator, but it could do sequences of calculations automatically by following instructions in a program. Since it could function automatically for many hours at a stretch, it could do the work of many people equipped with calculators.

THE ELECTRONIC DIGITAL COMPUTER

The relay computer could not compute very fast. The need was for a machine that was much, much faster. World War II greatly increased this need. For example, there was the need to calculate artillery firing tables for each batch of artillery ammunition that was produced. There was the need to keep track of huge stockpiles of war materials and payroll records needed to be kept for millions of service personnel.

In England, Alan Turing developed an electronic digital computer that was used to decode secret German war messages. In Germany, a scientist named Konrad Zuse developed an electronic digital computer. Then, starting in 1943, people began to build an electronic digital computer in the United States. It used vacuum tubes (similar to the tubes in old radios) in place of telephone-type relays. The design and construction work was done at the University of Pennsylvania under the supervision of J. Presper Eckert and John Mauchly.

The resulting machine became operational in December, 1945. It was called the ENIAC, and is considered to be the first general purpose electronic digital computer. It contained 18,000 vacuum tubes, and was more than a thousand times as fast as the Mark I relay computer.

The ENIAC was a massive machine. The 18,000 vacuum tubes generated a large amount of heat, so the computer had to be in an air conditioned room. Vacuum tubes burnt out regularly, so often the machine did not work properly. But when it did work right it could do the work of 1,000 people using calculators!

During the next few years many new ideas were developed on how to build better computers. John von Neumann was the first person to think of many of these ideas. (One of the early computers was actually called the JOHNNIAC.) Von Neumann is also known for helping to develop a field of study called game theory, and for many other contributions to the field of mathematics.

The first company to build computers for sale was Remington Rand Corporation. (This company is now part of Sperry Rand Corporation.) They called their computer the UNIVAC I, and first sold it in 1951. It wasn't until several years later that IBM began to be a leader in making and selling computers. IBM is now by far the largest computer company in the world. Indeed, it sells several times as many dollars worth of computer equipment each year as any one of its competitors.

MODERN COMPUTERS

Early electronic digital computers had two major flaws: they broke down quite often because vacuum tubes burnt out and they had small memories. The technology to solve both of these problems was developed during the late 1940s and early 1950s. the three key developments were:

1. The development of better primary storage (using something called magnetic "core" memory).

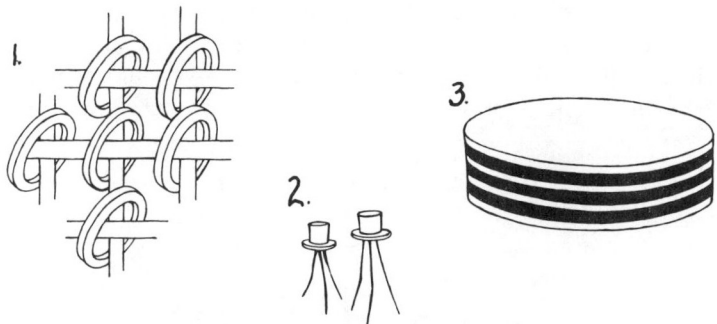

2. The development of the transistor which seldom burns out. (It replaced the vacuum tube.)
3. The development of magnetic disk and related ideas for secondary storage.

By the end of the 1950s, all of these inventions were being used in computers, and by 1960 we had computers that were quite fast, had large storage capacity, and were quite reliable. These computers, while powerful, were very expensive. Not too many schools or companies could afford to buy a machine costing many hundreds of thousands of dollars.

Since 1960 computer manufacturers have made steady progress in producing better computers at lower prices. The machines have become faster, more reliable, and physically smaller. Researchers at Texas Instruments Corporation discovered how to manufacture a circuit containing many transistors and other components all hooked together on a small chip of silicon. First they learned how to build a circuit containing a few dozen components. Soon they could put hundreds, and then thousands of components onto a chip less than 1 cm square.

It is such a chip (also called a large scale integrated circuit) that makes cheap calculators possible. Almost all of the circuitry for a pocket calculator is contained in one single chip. Chips for a simple 4-function calculator can be mass produced for less than a dollar apiece.

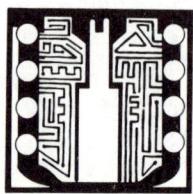

In the past few years continued progress has occurred. The circuitry for an *entire computer* has been built into a single chip! It is called a *microprocessor*, and many millions of them are being built. It has been estimated that by 1985 the average

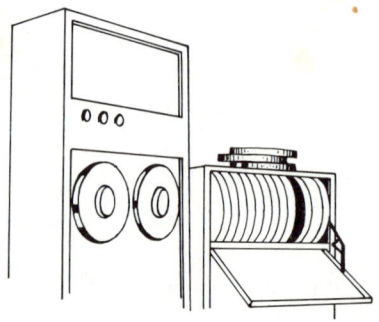

Why Do Computers Exist?

home will contain 10 to 20 microprocessors. These will be in cars, microwave ovens, dishwashers, clothes washers and dryers, television sets, record players, tape decks, etc. Battery powered games such as football and auto racing, which contain a microcomputer, now sell for $20 to $30. The age of computers is upon us!

The typical "home" computer consists of a microprocessor, a keyboard, a TV-like display screen, and a cassette tape recorder. The microprocessor may only cost $10 or so. Most of the cost of a microcomputer is for the power supply, primary and secondary memory, and input/output devices.

WHAT DO YOU CALL PEOPLE WHO COUNT ON THEIR FINGERS?

To find out, complete each statement by circling 1 of the 2 responses following it. Then match the letter in your response with each statement number and fill in the blanks below.

1. The first electronic computer used   transistors—H / vacuum tubes—I
2. The first mechanical aid to computing was the   slide rule—S / abacus—T
3. Which of these was invented earlier?   television—M / electronic computer—N
4. The person who used punched cards in the 1890 census was   Hollerith—U / Jacquard—I
5. The first general purpose electronic digital computer was built in the U.S. during   World War II—R / Space Program—M
6. The first electronic digital computer was called   ENIAC—S / UNIVAC I—T
7. A mathematician who also built a mechanical calculator was   Pascal—O / Descartes—A
8. The first mechanical calculators were mainly used by   scientists—A / mathematics students—E
9. The "relay" computer that used telephone circuitry was slower than those termed   mechanical—J / electronic—G
10. Major problems occured with the first electronic computer because of its   excessive cost—I / vacuum tubes—E

11. The largest computer company in the world now is   IBM—P
                                                             Sperry-Rand—Q
12. One common type of primary storage for modern computers consists of magnetic   tape drives—D
                                                             core units—C
13. Transistors in computers have replaced the use of   punched cards—M
                                                             vacuum tubes—L
14. Calculators have become cheaper because of an invention called   magnetic cards—B
                                                             chips—D

```
_ I _ I _ _ _     _ _ _ _ _ _ _ _ _ _ _
14 1 9 1 2 8 13   12 7 3 11 4 2 10 5 6
```

COMPUTER CARD CODES

Punched cards are still widely used for computer input. They are also used for computer output, and sent to people as bills.

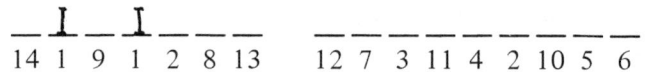

A computer "reads" the holes in a punched card. The holes are really codes for letters, digits, and punctuation marks. Each digit has a code that is a single hole. Each letter has a code that is two holes. Each punctuation mark has a code that is three holes. Notice that the card contains 80 columns. That is the total number of characters (digits, letters, and punctuation marks) that can be punched on one card.

The printing on the top of the first card allows you to see the code for each character. Often cards are punched without any printing along the top.

Look at a punched card bill at home, and see if you can figure out what is punched on it.

CHAPTER FOUR

DATA ENTRY AND COMPUTER PROGRAMMING

Data entry and computer programming are two of the key ideas about computers. Test your knowledge of this area by answering the following true-false questions.

T   F   (1) Punched cards are a very common method for inputting data to a computer.
T   F   (2) Magnetic ink is used for computer input of data from bank checks.
T   F   (3) An optical character recognition machine can read typewriter data.
T   F   (4) A computer can understand anything said to it in English provided the person doesn't speak too fast.
T   F   (5) The universal product code on a grocery store item contains the price of the item.
T   F   (6) A computer program is a detailed set of instructions telling a computer what to do to solve a particular type of problem.
T   F   (7) A very short computer program can sometimes be used to process a large amount of data.
T   F   (8) All computers understand BASIC, since it is the most basic of all programming languages.
T   F   (9) Nowadays, many junior high students learn to write computer programs.
T   F   (10) One must understand binary arithmetic and machine language in order to program a computer.

COMPUTER LIMITATIONS

In Chapter 2 we listed four general areas of computer limitations. We discussed two of them—speed, and storage capacity. We concluded that computers are very fast and can have very large storage capacity. Thus, for most applications, speed and storage capacity are not serious limitations.

The other two areas of concern are data preparation and program writing. The data to be processed must be put into a form that can be input to a computer. This can be a costly and time-consuming process.

If a problem is to be solved by a computer, someone must write a program that tells the computer exactly what to do. Figuring out how to write programs can be very difficult.

This chapter discusses various methods of getting data into a form so that it can be input to a computer. It also discusses some of the general ideas of computer programming.

DATA

Information to be processed by a computer is called *data*. It can take many forms. Sometimes it is numbers, such as air pressure readings radioed back by a weather balloon. Sometimes it is words, such as a book or newspaper to be typeset by a computer. Sometimes it is picture-type information, such as a television signal. Television pictures from the moon and from Mars were processed by computer to get clearer pictures.

Preparing data in a form so it can be input to a computer can be a large task. For many years, the most common way to prepare data for a computer was to punch it onto cards. The card punch machines used to punch the 1890 United States

Data Entry and Computer Programming

Census data were not electrically powered. Punching was a rather slow process, much like using a hand paper punch.

The modern keypunch machine is like an electric typewriter. Depressing a key on the keypunch causes a pattern of holes to be punched onto a card. A keypunch operator can punch cards about as fast as a typist can type. The same kinds of skills are involved.

Keypunching is slow and expensive if one has lots of data. Also, the keypunch person makes mistakes, and sometimes these mistakes don't get detected. This causes wrong data to go into the computer—and often this causes a computer to produce wrong answers. Most of the errors blamed on computers are actually due to errors in data entry.

For many years people have been looking for better ways to input data to a computer. We will discuss a few of them.

1. **Key to tape and key to disk:** It is now common to use an electric typewriter mechanism to key data onto magnetic tape or disk. This saves cards, and makes it easier to correct an error. A magnetic tape or disk can be erased, whereas a card with a wrong pattern of holes must be thrown away (recycled).

2. **Mark sense readers:** Probably you have taken true-false and multiple choice tests in which you marked the answer between little lines on a test scoring sheet. These sheets can be

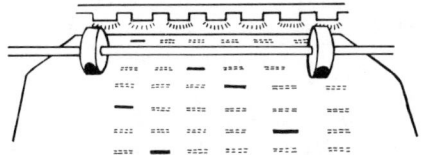

read by a mark sense reader. The mark sense reader can read a sheet and write the data onto magnetic tape or disk. This is a fast and cheap method to get data into computer-readable form; the person taking the test does much of the work!

3. **Magnetic ink:** Every bank check processed in the United States contains an account number. Each person's account number is different. The number is printed on the lower left hand corner of the check. It is printed using an ink containing small particles of iron, and using numbers of a special shape. Banks have machines that can read these magnetic ink numbers.

When a bank receives a check, it types the amount in magnetic ink on the lower right hand side of the check. Then a computer reads the account number and the amount of the check. The

computer keeps track of each person's checking account balance and prints out a summary statement for each account at the end of the month.

4. **Optical character recognition (OCR):** Much of the data people want to input to a computer is already printed or typed. For many years people have been trying to make computer input devices that could read printed and typewritten materials. Now such machines have been developed. They can read an entire page of print or typing in less than one second using a process called optical character recognition (OCR).

Right now some OCR machines can also read carefully hand-printed letters and numbers, but they cannot read most people's cursive handwriting. Sometime in the future it may be possible for OCR machines to read "messy" handwriting. This is a very difficult problem, since many people's handwriting is so bad that other *people* cannot read it. A solution in the next 5 to 10 years is unlikely.

5. **Universal product code (UPC):** Have you noticed that most grocery store items have a small pattern of dark bars on them? This is a coded form for two numbers. One number tells what company produced the item. The other is a product number.

Each product produced by the company has its own number. These numbers, called the universal product code (UPC), identify the grocery store item. The bar code can be read by a laser reading device, which inputs the numbers to a computer. The computer can look up the current price (from its memory) and thus total up the grocery bill. The computer can also be used to keep track of inventory this way.

6. **Voice input:** It would be very convenient if we could just talk to a computer, to give it data. Some voice input devices have been built, and are used in business and industry. They can

only understand a few words, and the words have to be spoken very carefully. In the future we can expect better and cheaper voice input devices. Right now voice input is not practical (because of cost and limited vocabulary) in very many applications.

7. **Sensing devices:** Much of the data input to computers comes from sensing devices. A TV camera on the moon or Mars takes pictures that are radioed directly to a computer located on Earth. A thermometer in a pot of melting steel measures the temperature and sends it to a computer. The computer controls the furnace that is heating the steel. An X-ray machine scans a patient and sends the data directly into a computer. These types of computer data input occur throughout industry and in scientific research. They are often a cheap way to get data into a computer.

COMPUTER PROGRAMMING

A computer program is a detailed, step by step set of directions telling a computer exactly how to solve a certain kind of problem. It must be written in a language that can be "understood" by a computer. The typical computer understands how to do about 100 to 200 different instructions. Different brands of computers have different instruction sets.

```
10  READ A
20  LET P=1.20 *A
30  PRINT "COST=";A,"PRICE =";P
40  GO TO 10
50  DATA 3.45, 2.89, 6.43, 2.48
60  END
```

Often (but not always) a computer's instruction set includes instructions to add, subtract, multiply, and divide numbers. Other instructions allow data to be moved from a card reader, magnetic tape, magnetic disk, or sensing devices into the computer's primary memory storage, while others allow the computer to place data (for example, answers) into secondary storage, or to output it on some sort of printing device. Many of the instructions in a computer's instruction set are used to move data between various parts of the machine, such as between primary storage and the place where arithmetic is done.

All computers have instructions that compare numbers. The computer can decide which of two different things it is to do, based upon the results of a comparison. This very important idea is illustrated in the flowchart given below. A flowchart is a two-dimensional picture showing a step by step set of directions. It is designed to be read by a person, and is sometimes used as an aid in writing a computer program. The flowchart given below directs a person to write down the numbers from 1 to 500.

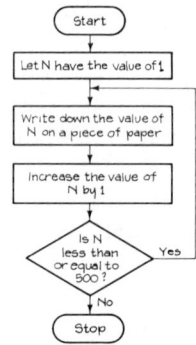

Flowcharts have been used by computer programmers for many years. Different shape boxes are used to help the reader follow the directions. Thus, the START and STOP boxes are oval shaped. The rectangular box is used to specify a computational task or action. The diamond box is used for decision questions. Arrows are used to help show the order in which the instructions are to be carried out.

Notice that while this flowchart is short, it directs a person to complete a very long task. By one small change to the flowchart, we can make it direct a person to write the numbers from 1 to 5000. Do you see what change to make? The important idea to remember is that a very short computer program can sometimes be used to process a very large amount of data.

A computer program written in the language BASIC is given below. When a computer executes this program, it will print out the numbers from 1 to 500. Note that there is a close relationship between the flowchart and the program.

```
10 LET N=1
20 PRINT N
30 LET N = N + 1
40 IF N<=500 THEN 20
50 STOP
60 END
```

BASIC stands for Beginners All-purpose Symbolic Instruction Code. It is a computer programming language that was designed to be easy for students to learn. It is the most widely used computer programming language at the pre-college level, and it can be used with many different brands of computers. Most inexpensive microcomputers can be programmed using BASIC.

The idea of a language such as BASIC is very interesting. It is a language designed to be read and used by people, but also to be used by computers. BASIC is not a "natural" language (like English, French, or Russian) and so people do not learn to speak it as they grow up. Instead, it is an artificial language with very precise rules of grammar and construction. People learn BASIC in order to be able to write precise instructions for a computer.

But computers do not understand BASIC directly. Computer circuitry works with electricity. Switches are *open* or *closed*. A spot on a magnetic storage device is *magnetized* or *not magnetized*. Current is *flowing* or *not flowing*.

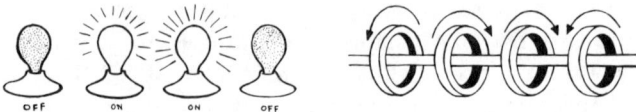

People use the symbols ∅ and 1 to denote the open/closed, on/off, magnetized/not magnetized ideas in a computer. Thus the binary number system, which uses just ∅'s and 1's, is the "alphabet" of computers. The machine language of a computer is designed to work with instructions and data coded as sequences of ∅'s and 1's.

If a computer is going to execute a program written in BASIC then somehow the BASIC instructions must be translated into the machine's language. This can be done by the computer itself, following the instructions given in a computer program called a *translator*. The rules for BASIC are so precise that a computer can translate from BASIC into a *machine language*.

Not all computers have the same machine language. Each model of computer that is to understand BASIC must have its own translator. A translator is a very complex program, usually supplied by the computer manufacturer. It may be many thousands of instructions in length.

There are many other widely used languages besides BASIC. In the world of business, the most commonly used language is COBOL. It was designed to make it easier to write programs to solve business problems. Other widely used programming languages include ALGOL, FORTRAN, PASCAL, and PL/1. Each of these languages requires its own translator.

We saw earlier that Roman numerals are useful, but are not as good as Hindu-Arabic numerals. The same idea holds for programming languages. As computer scientists learn more about computers they learn to make better programming languages. That is one reason why there are so many programming languages.

Another reason is that languages are designed to fit the needs of special groups of people. We said that BASIC was designed for students, and COBOL for business people. ALGOL and FORTRAN were designed mainly for scientists. PL/1 was designed to fit the needs of both business people and scientists. PASCAL was designed to fit the needs of computer scientists. Each language has certain features that make it extra good for solving certain types of problems.

Data Entry and Computer Programming

Learning to write computer programs is not very hard. Many grade school children have learned to program and programming is often taught at the junior high school level. Almost every large high school teaches it. But writing a program to solve a complex problem is hard work. It requires a person to understand exactly how to solve the problem in order to tell the computer how to do it. The computer is no substitute for thinking.

SUMMARY

If data is to be processed by a computer then it must be input to a computer. Data preparation can be an expensive and time-consuming task, but considerable progress has occurred in this area, and there are now many methods for getting data into a computer.

The most restrictive of the computer limitations is computer programming. A computer can only do what it is told to do. If a computer is to solve a problem, a person must first figure out how to solve the problem. Then a detailed program must be written. Progress in developing better programming language is occurring, which is a help to computer programmers. Also, computer scientists are making progress on helping people learn how to write programs. Thus we can expect that in the future more and more problems will be solved by computers.

HOW DID THE COMPUTER HELP CHASE DOWN THE CRIMINALS?

Match each statement with the best word on the right. No words are used twice. Not all words are used.

___1. Initially the most common way to input data to a computer.
___2. A machine that inputs data from test scoring sheets.
___3. Used on checks to read a person's bank account number.
___4. Pattern of bars on grocery store items.
___5. Industrial or scientific instruments that send data directly into computers.
___6. Step by step set of directions telling a computer exactly how to solve a problem.
___7. Two-dimensional picture showing a step-by-step set of directions.
___8. A computer programming language.

A magnetic ink numbers
B data
D sensing devices
E key punch cards
H BASIC
I output
M optical character recognition
N universal product code
T mark sense readers
U ENIAC
V integrated circuits
W program
X UNIVAC I
Y flowchart

Now place your answers below in the computer's reply.

IT TOLD THE LAW ENFORCEMENT OFFICERS:

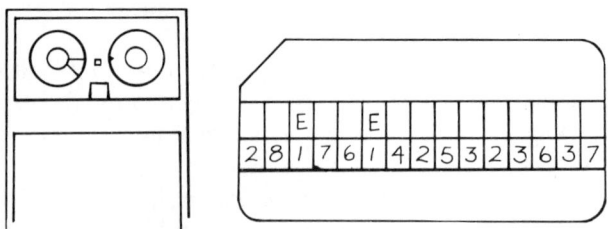

FOLLOW THE FLOWCHART

Quantities that are referred to by name, such as A, B and S, are called *variables*. Following a flowchart may involve keeping track of the value of each variable. A table such as the following is helpful. Complete the table for the numbers 8 and 3.

Data Entry and Computer Programming

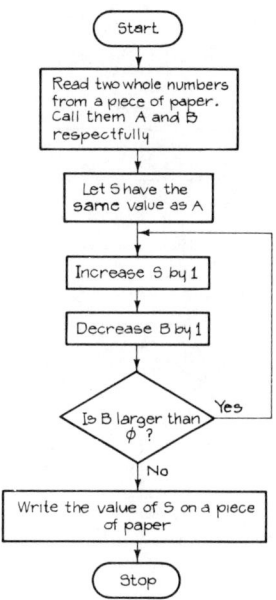

A	B	S
—	—	—
8	3	—
8	3	8
8	3	9

Start

Two numbers read

S given a value

S increased

B decreased

etc.

Make a table for the numbers 12 and 7.

What problem does the flowchart solve? What happens if the pair of numbers is 4 and 0?

An algorithm is a detailed step by step of directions. It is designed to solve a particular type of problem in a finite number of steps.

In school you learned an algorithm for adding a column of numbers. Make a list of algorithms that you know.

WORKING WITH WORDS

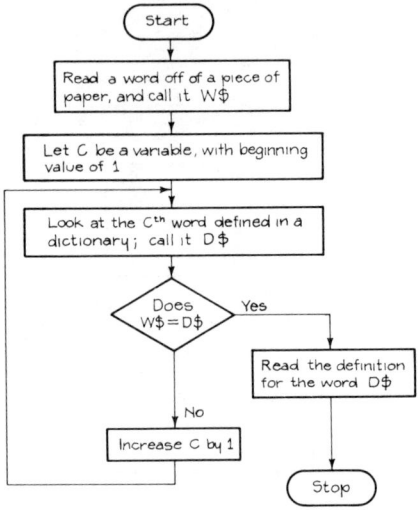

Follow the directions in the flowchart, where acid is the word read off the paper.

Workspace

W$	C	D$
Acid	—	—

Read word from paper

Let C = 1

Read first word
in dictionary

What happens if zebra is the word read from the paper? What happens if one tries to follow the flowchart for a word that is not in the dictionary?

Can you think of a faster way of looking up a word in a dictionary? Draw a flowchart to represent this faster method.

THE NUMBERS GAME

Here's a number trick to play on your friends. Make four cards like these shown:

C				O				D				E		
10	9	8		6	5	4		6	3	2		5	3	1
13	12	11		13	12	7		11	10	7		11	9	7
	15	14			15	14			15	14			15	13

Ask a friend to select a number from 1 to 15. Then tell the person you are going to guess the number. Hold up each card and ask if the number is on that card. After your friend's "yes" or "no" responses you should be able to guess the number.

Do you know how it works? The numbers game is based on the binary system. Think of the n's and y's standing for ∅'s and 1's. The binary place values are

	8	4	2	1
If your friend had picked the number *1* the responses should have been:	n	n	n	y
For the number ___6___	n	y	y	n
See if you can figure out these responses ___2___	n	n	y	n
___8___	y	n	n	n
___3___	n	n	y	y
___9___	y	n	n	y
___14___	y	y	y	n
_____	n	n	n	n
___15___	y	y	y	y

Try making up a 5 card game. This should allow any number from 1 to 31 to be guessed. Think of a 5 letter name for the cards.

DATA ENTRY PROBLEMS

A good key punch operator can punch about 15,000 characters per hour. If one punched card can contain 80 characters, how many full cards can a good key punch operator punch per 8 hour day? Roughly how long would it take such a person to key punch a million character book? (That is the length of a full length novel.)

A particular optical character recognition machine can read one typewritten page in 4 seconds. Suppose that a typical page contains 40 lines of typing, and an average line is 60 characters long. Express the speed of this OCR in characters per second. How long would it take this machine to read a million characters?

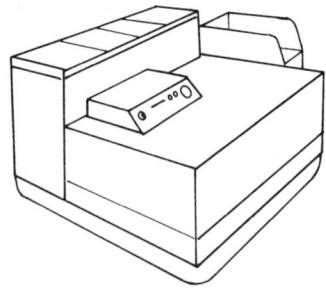

Each year in the United States about 30 billion checks are written and cashed. The amount of each check is keyed into the check, in magnetic ink, by a data entry person. Then a second person checks for errors by keying the data on a verifier. A verifier is a machine that compares what is being keyed with what was printed on the check by the first data entry person. Suppose that one person can key in the data from 6,000 checks in one working day. Remember that this means it takes two

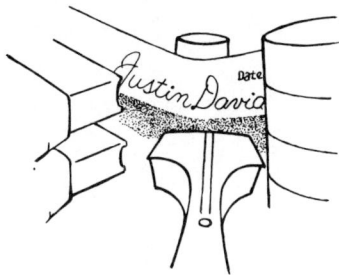

people to actually do the data entry on 6,000 checks in one day. Estimate the number of people who make their living keying in bank check data in the United States.

HOW FAST ARE YOU?

Make a set of 50 3×5 inch cards as follows. On one side of each card write a word of about 5 or 6 letters in length. These words should come from many different parts of a dictionary. On the other side of the card write a 5 or 6 digit number. The numbers selected should all be different.

Shuffle the cards and deal out 25 of them. Time yourself as you arrange those 25 in alphabetical order. Shuffle the same 25 cards again, and time the numerical ordering (from lowest to highest number).

Which is easier for you—alphabetical ordering or numerical ordering? Why do you think that this is the case?

Try the process with all 50 cards. Does it take more than twice as long?

Now write down a detailed step by step set of directions for alphabetizing a set of cards. A third or fourth grader should be able to understand these directions. Have a friend try to follow your written directions. Revise them until they can easily be read and followed by another student. Next write down some procedure for arranging the cards in increasing numerical order.

A computer can be programmed to alphabetize a set of words or to arrange numbers in increasing order. Computer programs can be written to follow the ideas you wrote down to order a set of cards. A modern computer can alphabetize a set of 50 words in a small fraction of a second.

SMART MACHINES

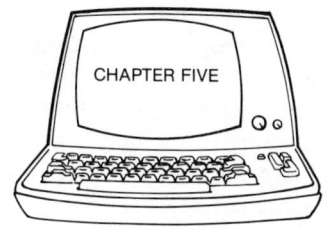

CHAPTER FIVE

Many process control machines and robot-like machines contain a built-in computer. See what you know about process control and robots by answering the following true/false questions.

T F (1) An automatic elevator could be classified as a "smart" machine.
T F (2) A thermostat is an example of a process control device.
T F (3) Nowadays every process control machine contains a built-in microprocessor.
T F (4) If a machine is to be classified as "smart" it must be at least as smart as an average first grader.
T F (5) X-ray equipment and a computer are used to control saws in some modern sawmills.
T F (6) In the typical home there are only one or two process control devices that might be replaced by microprocessors.
T F (7) Assembly line robots can do welding, screw nuts onto bolts, and push connectors together.
T F (8) Most robots are at least as smart as the average person.
T F (9) Once a robot has been told what to do it will overcome almost any obstacle to accomplish its task.
T F (10) Most factory robots understand and can speak a small number of English words.

SMART MACHINES

There are many machines that can automatically carry out a sequence of instructions and can cope with certain difficulties. An automatic elevator is a good example. It accepts input from passengers, moves to the right floors in a logical order, and automatically opens and closes its door. If the door starts to close on a person, the elevator senses the obstacle and opens up again.

An automatic elevator is a smart machine. In no sense does it have the intelligence of even a first grader, but it is smart enough to do its job. At one time most elevators required a human operator. The human could do many things that the automatic elevator cannot do. For example, the human operator could answer questions, carry on a conversation, and respond to requests to "hold the elevator!" The high costs of labor have caused human elevator operators to be replaced by automatic elevators.

There are many machines that could be made more automatic, or "smarter." Computers are very useful for helping to do this. The very cheap microprocessor makes it possible to build computers into lots of other machines and in the future we will have more and more smart machines.

PROCESS CONTROL

Thermostats measure temperature and automatically turn the heat on and off. Suppose the thermostat in a room is set at 20 degrees Celsius. If the furnace is not on and it is cold

Smart Machines

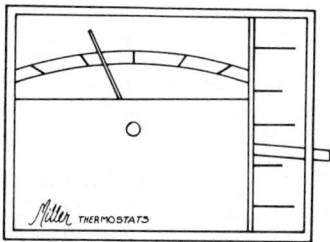

outside, the temperature will begin to drop. When it gets down to 19 or 18 degrees, the thermostat will "notice" that the temperature is too low and turn the heat on. The temperature will begin to rise and soon it will be up to 21 or 22 degrees. Now the thermostat will notice that the temperature is too high, and turn the heat off.

This is an example of process control. While most household thermostats do not contain microprocessors at the current time, many will in the future. In many large buildings, the thermostats send their temperature data to a computer. The computer controls the heat flow to the different rooms. Thus the heating control mechanism for the building is a smart machine.

The thermostat example illustrates the three key parts of a smart process control machine: 1) It must have some sort of measuring or sensing device in order to receive input from the outside world. 2) It must be able to use the data it receives. Here a computer is helpful, since it can perform computations on the data in order to decide what action is best. 3) It must be able to act upon the outside world.

Process control machinery is used in almost every factory. More and more of this machinery contains a built-in microprocessor, or is hooked to a larger computer. A typical application is in a steel mill. One task is to produce steel plates of a certain exact thickness. Gigantic rollers squeeze the steel to the correct thickness, while large gas heaters keep it hot. Computerized thickness gauges automatically measure the thickness and adjust the pressure on the rollers. Computerized thermometers measure the temperature of the steel and regulate the gas heaters.

Another example is in a modern sawmill. The goal is to make good use of all the wood in a log. An X-ray machine scans the log, and the data goes into a computer. The computer decides the best use of the log. It controls the saws, so that the log can

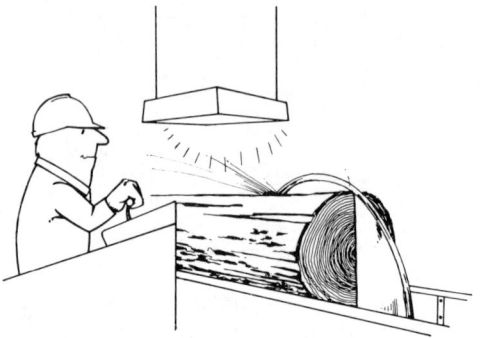

be cut in the right places. If finished lumber is desired, the computer avoids the knots as much as possible.

Still another application of smart machines is in traffic control. Sensing devices are built into the streets, or radar can be used to sense vehicles. This data is fed to the computer which then controls the traffic lights. If traffic starts to build up on one street, the computer can make the lights stay green longer on that street.

Think of all the measuring, timing, and control devices found around a home. Many can be replaced by small computers,

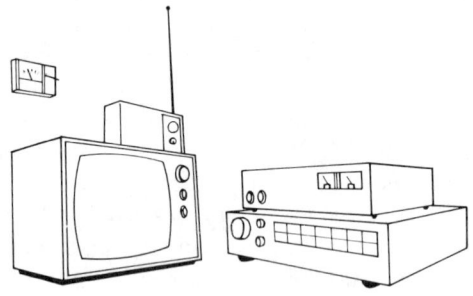

hence becoming smart machines. Within 10 years it will be common to find these small computers in automobiles, television sets, clock radios, thermostats, dishwashers, stereo hi-fi sets, stoves, washing machines, etc. You will benefit because your machines will cost less and/or run better. They will serve you better.

ASSEMBLY LINE ROBOTS

One of the key ideas of mass production is the assembly line. Workers sit or stand at their work stations, while parts to

Smart Machines

be assembled come to them. The worker does the same task over and over again. The worker almost becomes a machine.

For many years it has been clear that a machine can do many of the assembly line jobs. What is so hard about building a machine to perform the same welding task over and over? Why can't a machine push two connectors together, or screw some nuts onto bolts?

The answer is that a machine can be built for each of these tasks. But before computers, the machines had to be highly specialized. They could not easily adjust to a new task. Thus if the item being mass produced was to be changed, the assembly line machines had to be rebuilt.

Computers have changed this. Now it is possible to build an assembly line robot that can be programmed to do a particular job. To change it to a different job, one just changes the program. These assembly line robots do not walk or talk. They are just versatile machines that perform a certain task over and over again.

But such a robot does the work of a person, at a lower cost per hour. The robot can work two or three shifts per day and does not receive overtime pay. Of course the robot needs to be maintained, repaired, and programmed. This creates new jobs. Also, some people have jobs building robots. (Robots can work on the assembly lines that build new robots!) But the new jobs require higher levels of training and often they cannot be filled by the assembly line workers, and in total, a smaller number of workers are required.

ROBOT GAME NUMBER ONE

One can learn quite a lot about robots and computer programming by playing the robot games discussed in this section and the next section.

A delivery robot is used by some large businesses. It is a motorized cart that automatically moves between various desks on one floor of a very large office building. When it reaches a desk, it stops and says "bleep bleep." It waits a few seconds so the person working at the desk can put mail and packages onto the cart, or take some off. Then it automatically goes on to the next desk.

Select one person to play the role of robot, and you be the robot's "programmer." Your task is to direct the robot to carry a written message from one part of the room to another. Assume initially that the robot is standing facing you, as in the picture below.

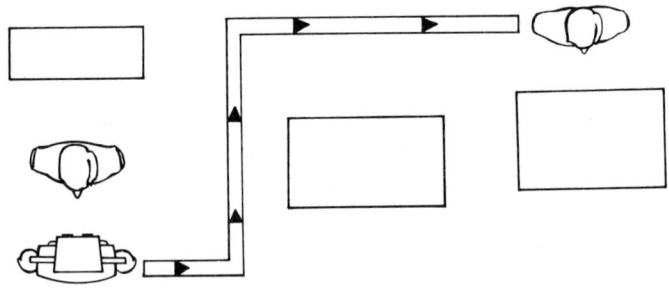

Your Instruction

1. Raise your right forearm until it is parallel to the floor and extended straight forward.
2. Prepare to grasp a piece of paper by opening a space between thumb and index finger.
3. Open up a space between thumb and index finger of right hand.
4. You now insert the written message into the robot's hand and give it the instruction: Close the thumb and index finger of right hand together.

Robot's Response

1. Robot raises right forearm as directed.

2. THAT DOES NOT COMPUTE! (The robot can't do this because you haven't said which hand.)

3. Robot opens right hand in a grasping position.

4. Robot grasps the piece of paper.

Smart Machines

5. Turn right ¼ of a full turn.	5. Robot turns right ¼ turn.
6. Take one step forward.	6. Robot takes one step forward.
7. Turn left ¼ of a full turn.	7. Robot turns left ¼ turn.
8. Etc., etc., etc.	

In directing the robot you must make sure that it does not run into a chair, desk, bookcase, or a person. Thus you must continually observe its location and figure out the consequences of what you are telling it to do.

Whenever you give an instruction that is not clear (such as "turn ¼ of a full turn") the robot is to respond THAT DOES NOT COMPUTE! Each instruction must be precise and it must have exactly one possible meaning.

After you have played this type of game for awhile, you will see the advantage of shortening the instructions. Thus you may want your robot to be constructed so that it can understand and carry out instructions such as the following:

Your Instruction	*Robot's Response*
1. Raise right forearm.	1. Robot raises right forearm by bending right arm at the elbow. The right forearm is to be parallel to the floor and extended straight forward.
2. Prepare right hand to grasp.	2. Robot opens right hand so there is a space between the thumb and index finger.
3. Grasp with right hand.	3. Robot grasps with thumb and index finger of right hand.
4. Turn right ¼ turn.	4. Robot turns right ¼ of a full turn.
5. Etc.	

The instructions used in computer programming languages are usually very brief. Thus it takes some effort to learn their precise meaning. That is part of what is involved in learning a programming language.

ROBOT GAME NUMBER TWO

In the first robot game the person directing the robot serves as its eyes, and continually observes the robot's location. Thus the programmer continually adjusts the robot's program, to keep the robot from doing something wrong. But the robot really isn't very useful if a person has to follow it around and tell it exactly what to do at each step.

We can get around this by adding some sensing devices to our robot. We can give it a television camera or a radar set for an eye, and a sense of touch.

With these features we can program our robot in advance, so that it can automatically carry out an assigned task. Some examples of this are given in the following piece of a program. The idea is that the robot receives the entire program in advance, and stores it in its memory. When told to GO it then carries out the program.

Program Step	*Comments*
1. Raise right forearm.	
2. Prepare right hand to grasp.	
3. Signal.	Robot goes "bleep bleep" to attract a person's attention.
4. Wait 14 seconds.	During this time the person is to insert the paper into the robot's hand and hold it there until robot grasps.
5. Grasp.	
6. Turn right ¼ turn.	
7. Is pathway clear for one step?	Robot examines pathway in front of itself, using its eye. Result is a "yes" or "no" answer that is stored in its memory.
8. If "yes" go to step 12. Otherwise go to step 9.	
9. Signal.	Robot goes "bleep bleep" to attract someone's attention.
10. Wait 5 seconds.	The robot then waits for the obstacle to be removed, and tries again.

Smart Machines

11. Go to step 7.
12. Take one step forward.
13. Etc.

As you can see, programming a robot such as this requires careful and detailed thought. Also notice how stupid the robot actually is. Suppose that the picture is as follows:

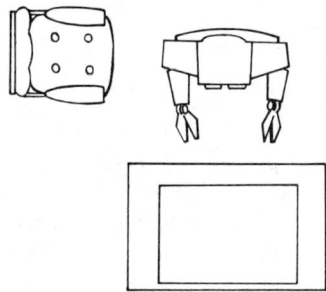

The robot following the program extends its forearm and prepares to grasp. But there is no person there to give the robot a piece of paper. The robot grasps (nothing) and turns right. But now a chair is in its pathway. It goes "bleep bleep" and waits 5 seconds. Then it goes "bleep bleep" and waits 5 seconds. Then it goes "bleep bleep" and waits 5 seconds . . . Our robot will continue to do this until its power source is exhausted.

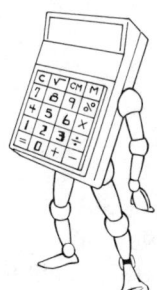

SUMMARY

Most "smart" machines are not very smart. But they can carry out the tasks they are designed to do. Often a task is one that used to be done by human workers. The smart machine replaces a human worker in order to cut down costs. But it also may put a person out of a job. This is a difficult problem that society must face. It is also a problem that *you* may face some day. Chapter 7 discuss that topic in more detail.

HAVE YOU READ?

FRANKENSTEIN

Many of you know about Frankenstein's monster, the robot-like creature in Mary Godwin Shelley's famous story. After the monster is invented, he becomes dangerous and destroys his master. Since that time many short stories, particular science fiction stories, have been written about robots.

R.U.R

Do you know where the word "robot" came from? Karl Capek made up the word to describe the artificial people in his play written in 1923. The play, called *R.U.R*, is about an inventor who manufactures millions of "Rossum's Universal Robots" to sell all over the earth. The robots decide to take control and do away with people! But by the end of the story, two of the robots change and start to take on human characteristics.

I, ROBOT

Robots and androids (robots that look like humans) are very common in modern science fiction. *I, Robot*, by Isaac Asimov is

Smart Machines 65

a collection of stories about robots and the future of "robotics." One of the stories lists and discusses the three laws of robotics. These laws, made up by Isaac Asimov, allow robots to be useful to people but prevent them from being a danger to people.

Science fiction stories about robots are fun to read, and they stimulate the imagination. Often they prove to be good predictions of the future. Science fiction stories sometimes contain serious messages about our current society. You may learn a lot about people while reading a story about robots.

* Make up a set of "laws" that you think all robots should obey. Write a short explanation of the purpose of each of your laws.
* Find out Isaac Asimov's three laws of robotics. Compare them with the laws you made up. Can you find flaws in either set of laws?
* Read a short story or book in which an android or robot is a main character. Discuss the social or "human" message the story is trying to convey.
* Check to see if your library has the three previous stories or any of these:

"Maxon's Master," by Ambrose Bierce
"I, Robot," by Eandro Binder (a different story from Asimov's)
"Who Can Replace A Man?" by Brian W. Aldiss
"Men Are Different," by Alan Bloch

ARE THESE SMART MACHINES?

Many machines now have small computers built into them. The small computer, or microcomputer, is used to help the machine make complicated decisions. It does this by analyzing lots of input (data) and looking at the many alternatives for the machine.

A smart machine usually has three parts:

1. a sensing device for input
2. an ability to use data it receives
   (through microprocessors)
3. a way to act on the outside world

Look at the devices below and decide which are apt to be smart machines.

Shade the regions that do *not* contain smart machines.

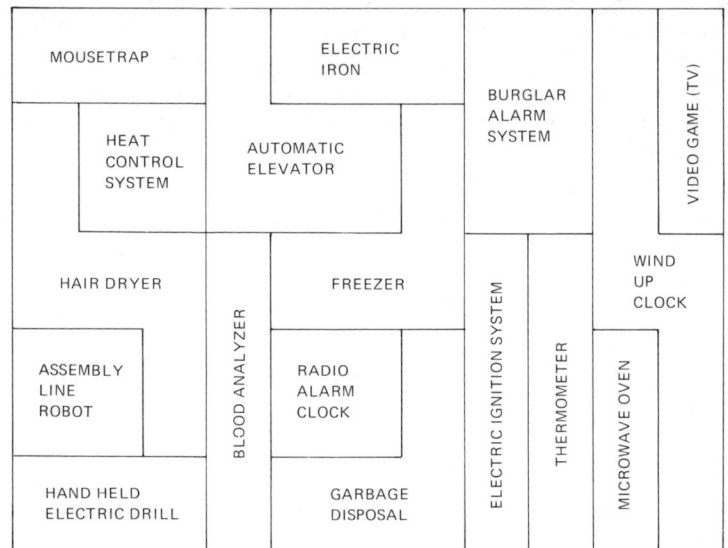

Turn your paper around for a response!

COMPUTERS AND SOCIETY

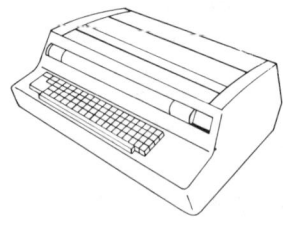

SMART TYPEWRITERS

An ordinary typewriter would probably not be classified as a smart machine. But nowadays many typewriters have microprocessors built into them, and are hooked to large (secondary storage) memory devices. Form letters and commonly used paragraphs can be stored in the computer memory. How do you think such computerized typewriters affect a typist's productivity? Make a list of the things you think a smart typewriter should be able to do. Do you think a smart typewriter could detect spelling errors? Discuss some difficulties involved in detecting and correcting spelling errors.

SORTING MACHINES

At one time all sorting of mail was done by hand. Now the postal system makes extensive use of automated sorting machinery. Envelopes move on a conveyer belt past a clerk who reads the zip code. The clerk keys the zip code into the sorting machine, which then places the letter into the correct bin. This is much faster than sorting by hand, but it may not be as accurate. How has this machine affected the number of postal jobs?

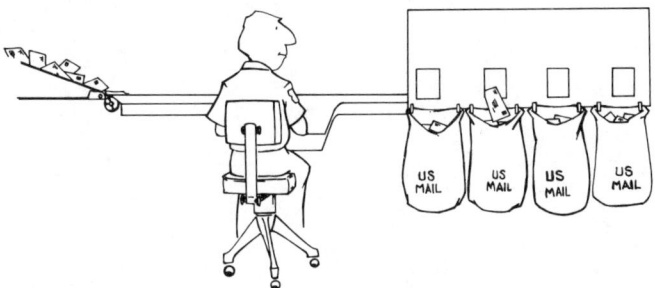

One can now buy machinery that can read typewritten numbers. If all letters had their zip codes typed in a prescribed spot, a machine could both read and sort letters by zip code. How do you think people would react to a law requiring all letters to contain typewritten zip codes? How would people who did not own a typewriter be able to use the mail service?

HOW COMPUTERS ARE BEING USED

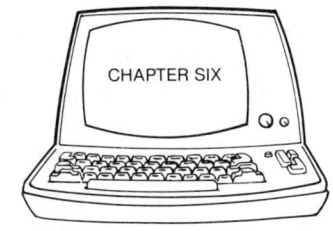

CHAPTER SIX

This chapter discusses more general uses of a computer. Check yourself to see how much you already know.

T F (1) Most school districts make considerable use of computers.
T F (2) Computer simulations are fun to do but are usually not helpful to anyone.
T F (3) Most computer time is spent in just doing mathematics.
T F (4) Some doctors use computers now to help diagnose a patient's illness.
T F (5) A formula such as A = B × H could be considered a mathematical model.
T F (6) Major airlines haven't started using computers yet.
T F (7) Information retrieval is the largest general use of computers.
T F (8) Computers can be used to produce pictures.
T F (9) Information retrieval could involve looking up the prices of grocery items if they are marked with the Universal Product Code.
T F (10) Full text searching is generally done by a microprocessor, with the text being stored on a cassette tape.

HOW COMPUTERS ARE USED

In Chapter 1 we listed many different uses of computers. We could continue that list. Did you know, for example, that many secretaries use computers to increase their output of typing? In a word processing system an electric typewriter is attached to a small computer which has enough memory to store a number of pages of typing. The computer also stores paragraphs from form letters. Typed material can be viewed on a small TV screen, checked for errors, and corrections made. After there are no more errors, the word processing system types out a copy, at a very high speed, on paper. Word processing increases a secretary's productivity.

We could also spend more time discussing computer uses that you probably already know about. Many of the math problems that people try to solve involve computation. A calculator or a computer can be used to do these computations. Indeed, the first computers were designed just for doing math. But nowadays there are many uses of computers outside of math, and most computer usage does not involve solving math problems.

In Chapter 5 we used a different approach to discuss uses of computers. We selected a broad category of uses (process control) and then discussed it. This helps to tie the main ideas together. In this chapter we will look at some other general categories of computer uses.

MODELING

Before we can discuss the next main category of computer usage we need to understand the idea of modeling. As a child you may have played with and built model cars, trains, airplanes, and houses. These models have some of the features of the "real thing," but they are smaller, simpler, cheaper, easier to build, and easier to modify.

Scientists and engineers often use scale models. A scale model of an airplane or rocket ship can be tested in a wind tunnel to help determine how the full scale product will perform. Similarly, an architect will often build a scale model of the office

building he or she is planning, to allow people to see how the final building will look, and how it will fit in with its surroundings.

Sometimes one does not need a physical scale model—a picture of the model may be all that is needed. But how can one get a picture of a model without building the model? That is not hard. One can have an artist draw it. Or, one can have a computer draw it. A graphics terminal uses a display screen like a TV screen and a computer that has been programmed to draw pictures. If a color TV screen is being used, the pictures can be in color.

Engineers and architects make frequent use of computer graphics terminals. The computer and its terminal have become part of their drawing and model displaying equipment. Parts of a drawing can be added or easily erased. Parts can be enlarged, shrunk, or viewed from a different angle. After the "drawing" is completed on the graphics terminal, a copy of it can be printed onto paper by the computer.

MATHEMATICAL MODELING

Mathematical models are very important in all branches of science. Have you ever seen the formula $E = mc^2$? This is a mathematical model which relates matter and energy. It was developed by Albert Einstein and it helps explain how an atomic bomb works.

Do you remember the meaning of the formual $A = \pi r^2$? It is a math formula (that is, a mathematical model) that relates the area and radius of a circle. It holds true for all circles.

Math is at the very heart of much of science, and mathematical modeling is one of the key ideas. Much of what scientists "know" are models that describe what they think is true. Consider, for example, the model $d = .5gt^2$. It gives the distance an object will move in time t under the influence of a gravity pull

g. This model can be applied to objects on the earth, the moon, or Mars. It is important because it unifies (ties together) many ideas about how objects move under the influence of gravity.

Mathematical models are also used in the social sciences. An example is a model of our economy. What will happen to inflation and unemployment if income taxes are lowered? How will exports and imports be affected by a change in import duties? Economists have constructed mathematical models of our economy using very complicated formulas. They can be used to help answer questions like those listed above.

COMPUTER SIMULATION

Many of the mathematical models from science and social science are very complicated. They involve working with many numbers, many variables, and equations that are too difficult for people to solve by hand. These mathematical models require the use of computers. A computer program for a mathematical model is called a computer simulation. Computer simulation is a standard tool for people who want to use complex models.

Let's look at a simple example. Suppose you are a city traffic engineer. Lots of people are complaining about the one-way streets, the timing of traffic lights, and the traffic jams. You have some ideas on how to correct things. If 7th, 9th, and 11th Streets could be made two-way streets . . . If the traffic lights on E Street could stay green for an extra 8 seconds . . . If parking were not allowed on the south side of W Street . . . .

But how do you *know* if these things will help? Maybe they will make things worse. It costs a lot of money and takes a lot of time and energy to make these changes, so you don't want to try unless you are very sure they will help.

Computer simulation is a solution. A mathematical model can be built to show the streets, direction of traffic, timing of traffic lights, amount of traffic, etc. This is a difficult task, requiring well-trained traffic engineers and computer programmers, but if a good model can be built and simulated on a computer, then your questions can be answered. You can try out all of the proposed changes in the computer simulation. You can see if they cut down on the (simulated) traffic jams. You can experiment with other people's suggestions.

Computer simulation is a very powerful tool in many fields. The businessman wants to know what will happen to profits if he makes certain changes in his company. The weatherman wants to know what will happen to the weather if a very large dam is built, or a large area of desert is irrigated. An astronaut wants to know what will happen if a certain part of his ship malfunctions during a trip to the moon. In all of these cases, computer simulations have been developed. They help to answer the "what if . . . " questions.

INFORMATION RETRIEVAL

What do you do when you are reading and come to a word you do not know? Maybe you ask a friend for its meaning or maybe you look it up in a dictionary. People and books are sources of information. Using them is an example of information retrieval.

Learning to retrieve information is a very important aspect of schooling. You learn to look up the spelling and meaning of words in a dictionary. You learn to look up population figures and the location of cities and countries in an atlas. You learn to look up information about people, places, and things in an encyclopedia and in other books.

In recent years, computers have become a more and more important aid to information retrieval. Let's look at a simple example. You are interested in flying from Los Angeles to New York City three weeks from today. You call up a travel agency and ask about flights. The travel agent uses a terminal attached to a computer to see what flights are scheduled between Los Angeles and New York City. (Or the same information can be looked up in a book.) The computer (or book) also indicates the cost of the trip.

So you decide you would like to take the 1:30 P.M. flight. Are there any openings? This is where the computer excels. The travel agent types in the desired flight number, and the computer retrieves the information as to whether the flight is full. If the flight is not full, the agent types in your name, address, and phone number. The computer keeps track of all people holding tickets on the flight. Travel agents from throughout the world can use terminals to get flight information from this computerized data bank, allowing them to sell tickets for the flights without fear of overbooking.

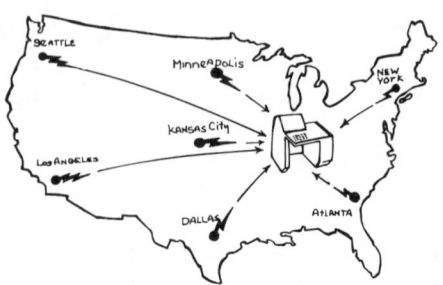

In the United States alone there are thousands of scheduled airline flights each day. Keeping track of all ticket sales for months in advance is a major task, and the airlines all depend upon computers to accomplish it.

There are many other information retrieval systems that work on the same ideas as the airline ticket reservation system. Police and FBI files are an example. Records are kept on the license numbers of stolen cars, the names of "wanted" people, and descriptions of other stolen property. When a police officer stops a speeding car, the officer radios in the license number. A computerized information retrieval system is used to check if this is a stolen car. The information is radioed back to the officer in just a few seconds.

Another example is provided by the UPC (Universal Product Code) and computerized grocery stores' checkout system we discussed in an earlier chapter. The current price and inventory information are stored in a computer memory. When a customer buys an item the laser input device reads the UPC and sends this information to the computer. The computer looks up the price

and rings it up on the cash register. The computer also subtracts one from the inventory count. All of this is done in a small fraction of a second.

There is another entirely different kind of information retrieval that makes use of computers. Consider the problem faced by a doctor trying to keep up with changes in the field of medicine. Each year about 300,000 new articles are published in medical journals. If a doctor tried to read all of these, there would be no time to treat any patients.

Suppose the doctor is examining a patient and decides that the patient may have a certain rare disease. The doctor would like to know the latest research results and treatment, but this would require subscription to thousands of medical journals.

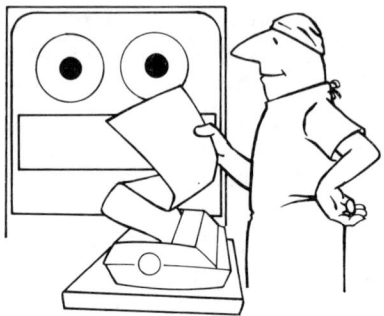

Even if all of the journals were available, it might not be obvious which articles were the most recent.

The computer provides an answer. Every medical article is indexed and a short summary is written. The index and summary are put into a computerized information retrieval system. Doctors from throughout the country can use keyboard terminals to retrieve information. The doctor just needs to type in the name of the disease, and the computer will give him the most recent references. If he wants, the computer will give him brief summaries of the articles. If the doctor needs to read the entire article he can look it up in a nearby medical library or he can order a copy of the article (the computer processes the order). A photocopy of the article is made and mailed out the next day.

This type of information retrieval is used in many other fields, such as biology, chemistry, education, engineering, physics, and psychology. It is beginning to have an effect upon libraries. It is now common to find a computer terminal in a college or university library, with librarians trained in its use. Some day it may be common to have a computer terminal in one's home, to use for information retrieval and other things. The British are now experimenting with such a system, and expect that it soon will be widely used in England.

One problem with information retrieval is that each article must be indexed and summarized. An alternative is to place the entire article into the information retrieval system. The computer then searches entire articles for desired words or phrases. This is called *full text searching*. Full text searching requires very large secondary storage and fast computers. But *large* modern computers have both of these features at a very reasonable cost. It is now practical to do full text searching and eventually it will become quite common. Lawyers currently make extensive use of full text searching on state and federal laws and on transcripts of some trials. Eventually entire libraries will be stored in computer secondary storage devices.

DATA PROCESSING

The last general category of computer usage we will look at is also the largest. It is known as business data processing, or simply as *data processing*. Data processing has to do with the collection, storage, and processing of data to produce needed reports. Earlier we discussed the use of punched card equipment to process the United States Census data of 1890. In the first half of the 20th century businesses made more and more use of punched card equipment for data processing.

In the early days of computers people did not think about using them for data processing. But the first UNIVAC I computer, sold in 1951, was sold to the United States Census Bureau. This part of the government was an early leader in use of computers for data processing.

But one does not need to examine the federal government to see computers being used for data processing. Most school districts and local governments make considerable use of computers. We will look at school use in more detail.

It takes a lot of money to run a school system. Teachers, janitors, clerks, administrators, cooks, coaches, bus drivers, and maintenance people must all be paid. Books, supplies, and food must be purchased. Thus the school system must keep good financial records and must issue many financial reports. The pay check a person receives is an example of a financial report. It tells him exactly how much take home pay he receives for the

pay period. A much more complicated report must be prepared by the central school office. It must contain the amount of local, state, federal, and social security taxes withheld for each person, and the totals for the school system. It must contain details on each person's work record, sick leave and accumulated retirement benefits.

Another area suited to use of compuers is student records. The school system needs to keep a lot of information about each student: name, date of birth, grade in school, parents' names and addresses, student medical history, student attendance and grade records, etc. Each term the teachers turn in

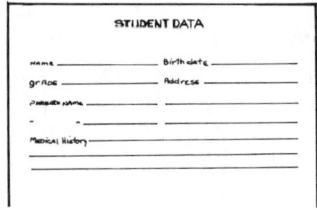

grades or credits for each student. These must be added to the central files, and grade reports must be issued to students (and/or parents). Schools must also submit attendance reports to the state government in order to get financial support from the state.

A third area of computer usage in the schools is for inventory. A school system must keep track of its textbooks, library materials, films, desks, chairs, school supplies, food supplies,

How Computers are Being Used

etc. This is quite similar to the problem faced by any large business. Some of the inventory items get used up in a regular manner. Others get lost, stolen, or worn out. A computer is a useful tool when one must keep track of a large number of items.

CONCLUSION

A computer is a machine for the input, storage, manipulation, and output of data. Some computer uses require much data manipulation, such as solving complicated mathematics problems. Other applications work with large amounts of data, such as in information retrieval, or business data processing.

We have not covered all of the major uses of computers. For example, one of the important uses we have left out is using computers to teach. One can think of this as using a computer to simulate the teaching process, or one can think of it as a form of information retrieval. Certain aspects of it involve keeping detailed records of a student's progress. This could be considered to be an example of data processing. In any event, you should now understand that there are many, many uses of computers. In the next chapter we will see how some of them may affect you.

WHAT DO YOU GET WHEN YOU CROSS A COMPUTER WITH A GORILLA?

Select the best answer for each of these multiple choice questions, then write the letter in the space provided.

_R_ 1. Student class schedules prepared by computer: (R) save administrative time and reduce scheduling conflicts; (S) make better teaching possible; (T) permit schools to accept more students.

___ 2. A researcher who has direct access to computer stored information will get: (R) answers to all of his or her questions; (S) immediate reference to the information; (T) improved working conditions.

___ 3. Most computers understand programs written in: (M) our natural English language; (N) any programming language; (O) specific programming language.

___ 4. Data-processing jobs performed by computers for business: (D) must be very simple; (E) may be simple or complex, with endless variety; (F) must be related to sales or cash payments.

___ 5. One of the drawing and model displaying tools is the: (X) storage or memory device; (Y) graphics terminal; (Z) central processing unit.

___ 6. A computer program for a mathematical model is called: (A) a computer simulation; (B) a computer library; (C) artificial intelligence.

___ 7. The use of terminals to get information from a computerized data bank is called: (M) artificial intelligence; (N) information retrieval; (O) computer simulation.

___ 8. Full text searching refers to : (F) the process librarians use to retrieve lost books; (G) a student studying for a final exam; (H) the computer looking over entire articles for desired words or phrases.

Now put your answers on the corresponding numbers below, as in the example.

__	__	_R_	_R_	__	_R_	__	__	__	__	__	__	__
6	8	6	1	1	5	1	4	6	2	3	7	4	1

COMPUTER HAIKU

Haiku is a form of Jananese poetry. Two examples follow.

All pure in the leaves
I seize pale buds in the hills
Swish the leaf has blown

All black in the fog
I flash red trees in the mist
Look the moon has shrunk

These poems were composed by a computer. Notice that haiku is written with 17 syllables in 3 lines (5 in the first line, then 7, then 5). The Japanese poems are always about nature and give clues to the season or time of day.

Study the two poems above. What words are the same in each of them? Notice that the poems follow the patterns given below. A$ to I$ represent words to be filled in.

All A$ in the B$
I C$ D$ E$ in the F$
G$ the H$ has I$

A computer can write haiku by selecting words from a table provided by the computer programmer. An example of a table of suitable words is given below.

A$	B$	C$	D$	E$	F$	G$	H$	I$
Pure	Leaves	See	Round	Grass	Hills	Shoo	Flower	Dimmed
Black	Heat	Seize	Pale	Trees	Mist	Swish	Moon	Shrunk
Red	Fog	Smell	Red	Buds	Dusk	Look	Leaf	Sprung
Blue	Cold	Flash	Green	Hills	Heat	Crash	Bird	Blown

The first "computer generated" haiku at the top of the page comes from the number sequence 1, 1, 2, 2, 3, 1, 2, 3, 4. That is, the computer selects the first word from the A$ column, the first word from the B$ column, the second word from the third column, and so on.

*What number sequence was used to generate the second poem?

*What poem is generated by the number sequence 4, 3, 2, 1, 2, 3, 4, 3, 2?

*Add two more words to each column of the word table. Since each column now contains six words, a die can be tossed to select a random word. Use throws of a die to generate a haiku. Does your poem make sense?

A COMPUTER GALLERY

PART I

Many artitsts are now using the computer as a tool to produce pictures or sculpture. Sometimes machines help the artist to develop an idea, or they may help produce the actual printed copy.

A typical figure is shown in Figure 1. These are designed very much like those done on an ordinary typewriter, using the keyboard characters.

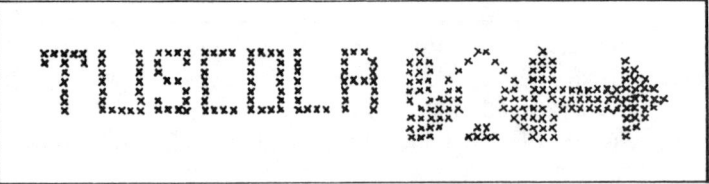

Figure 1

Design a simple picture on the grid. Try repeating letters to make a *giant* set of initials or simple shapes like triangles.

Besides the hard copy keyboard terminal and the line printer, there are two other devices used to produce pictures or prints. In all cases, a program must be written, giving the computer *very* specific instructions for output. The programming takes a long time compared to the speed with which the picture is drawn. Statements can be changed to vary a picture and the

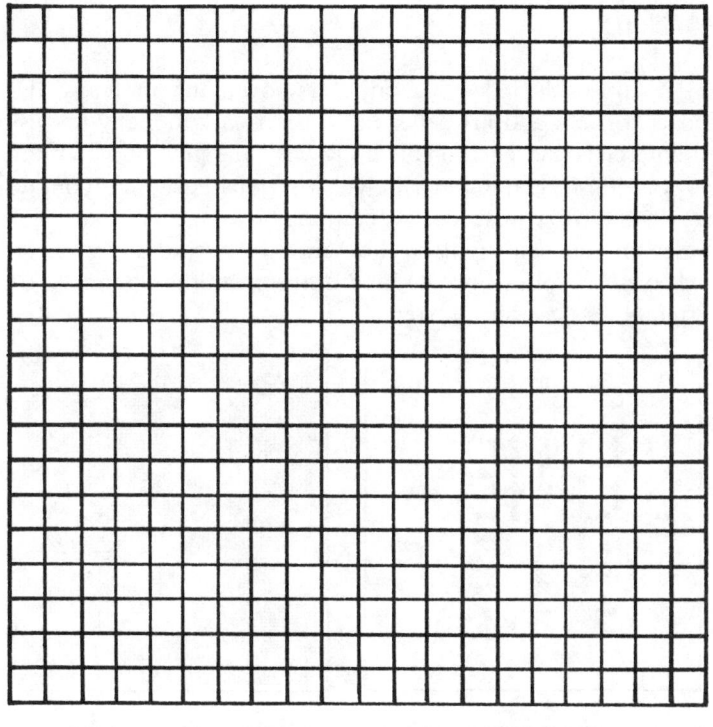

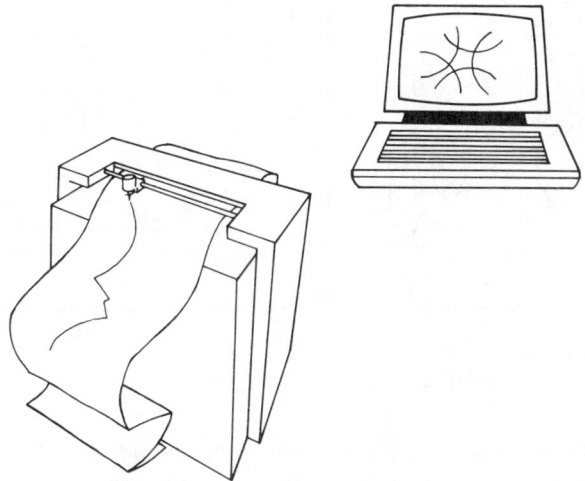

program can be re-run to make as many copies as desired. What are the advantages of producing pictures this way? What are some of the disadvantages?

PART II

Pictures plotted by computer now hang in many living rooms, offices and art galleries. The artwork in many television commercials and cartoons is done with the help of a computer. Do you think graphic artists will lose jobs because a computer can do the work instead? Explain your reasons.

See if you can identify the forms of output shown here as one of the following: keyboard terminal (hard copy), CRT terminal, lineprinter, plotter.

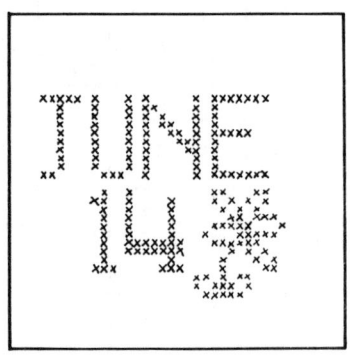

COMPUTER SIMULATIONS

Simulations can be run on almost any computer. One of the best known collections of educational simulations is called the Huntington simulations, developed by Ludwig Braun, under a grant from the National Science Foundation.

One of the Huntington simulations is called USPOP. It allows one to see how the United States population would change over a period of years, for various beginning situations and fertility rates. In the sample output given, the population begins at 204.8 million in 1970. The fertility rate starts at 2.45. The program user has indicated that the fertility is to change to 2.0 by 1980. With this fertility rate the population should stabilize. Study the sample output from the USPOP program.

```
DO YOU WANT REPORTS 1)EVERY 5 YEAR INTERVAL OR
2)SELECTED YEARS?1

YEAR AT START OF PROJECTION ?1970

DO YOU ASSUME STANDARD FERTILITY (1=YES,0=NO) ?1
WILL FERTILITY (1)STAY AT 2.45 OR (2) CHANGE SLOWLY
TO A NEW LEVEL ?2
WHAT FERTILITY WILL BE STABLE ?2.0
HOW MANY DECADES UNTIL FERTILITY REACHES 2 ?1

DO YOU ASSUME STANDARD BIRTH DISTRIBUTION (1=YES,0=NO) ?1

DO YOU ASSUME STANDARD SEX RATIO (1=YES,0=NO) ?1

DO YOU ASSUME STANDARD MORTALITY (1=YES,0=NO) ?1

DO YOU ASSUME STANDARD POPULATION (1=YES,0=NO) ?1

REPORT: 1)SHORT 2)LONG 3)GRAPH 4)CHANGE ASSUMPTION 5)END ?3


YEAR 1970    POP= 204.8 MILLION        FERTILITY 2.45
                    PCT. TOTAL POP.

            0........5........10........15........20
   0 -  4   .                :
   5 -  9   .                  :
  10 - 14   .                 :
  15 - 19   .               :
  20 - 24   .              :
  25 - 29   .            :
  30 - 34   .          :
  35 - 39   .        :
  40 - 44   .         :
  45 - 49   .         :
  50 - 54   .        :
  55 - 59   .      :
  60 - 64   .       :
  65 - 69   .    :
  70 - 74   .   :
  75+       .      :
```

```
YEAR 1980      POP= 222.8 MILLION      FERTILITY 2
                   PCT. TOTAL POP.

             0........5........10........15........20
   0 -  4  .              ::
   5 -  9  .              ::
  10 - 14  .              ::
  15 - 19  .             ::
  20 - 24  .             ::
  25 - 29  .            ::
  30 - 34  .           ::
  35 - 39  .          ::
  40 - 44  .          ::
  45 - 49  .        ::
  50 - 54  .         ::
  55 - 59  .         ::
  60 - 64  .       ::
  65 - 69  .      ::
  70 - 74  .    ::
  75+      .      ::


YEAR 1990      POP = 240.9 MILLION     FERTILITY 2
                   PCT. TOTAL POP.

             0........5........10........15........20
   0 -  4  .             ::
   5 -  9  .             ::
  10 - 14  .             ::
  15 - 19  .             ::
  20 - 24  .           ::
  25 - 29  .            ::
  30 - 34  .             ::
  35 - 39  .            ::
  40 - 44  .          ::
  45 - 49  .        ::
  50 - 54  .       ::
  55 - 59  .      ::
  60 - 64  .      ::
  65 - 69  .     ::
  70 - 74  .    ::
  75+      .     ::


YEAR 2000      POP = 255.4 MILLION     FERTILITY 2
                   PCT. TOTAL POP.

             0........5........10........15........20
   0 -  4  .             ::
   5 -  9  .             ::
  10 - 14  .              ::
  15 - 19  .              ::
  20 - 24  .             ::
  25 - 29  .             ::
  30 - 34  .             ::
  35 - 39  .            ::
  40 - 44  .              ::
  45 - 49  .        ::
  50 - 54  .         ::
  55 - 59  .       ::
  60 - 64  .      ::
  65 - 69  .     ::
  70 - 74  .    ::
  75+      .       ::
```

How Computers are Being Used

```
YEAR 2010      POP= 267.9 MILLION        FERTILITY 2
               PCT. TOTAL POP.

          0........5........10........15........20
 0 -  4 .          ::
 5 -  9 .          ::
10 - 14 .          ::
15 - 19 .           ::
20 - 24 .          ::
25 - 29 .           ::
30 - 34 .           ::
35 - 39 .         ::
40 - 44 .          ::
45 - 49 .         ::
50 - 54 ..         ::
55 - 59 .       ::
60 - 64 .        ::
65 - 69 .     ::
70 - 74 .    ::
75+     .      ::


YEAR 2020      POP= 278 MILLION          FERTILITY 2
               PCT. TOTAL POP.

          0........5........10........15........20
 0 -  4 .         ::
 5 -  9 .         ::
10 - 14 .         ::
15 - 19 .         ::
20 - 24 .         ::
25 - 29 .          ::
30 - 34 .          ::
35 - 39 .           ::
40 - 44 .         ::
45 - 49 .        ::
50 - 54 .        ::
55 - 59 .          ::
60 - 64 .        ::
65 - 69 .     ::
70 - 74 .   ::
75+     .    ::


YEAR 2030      POP= 282.1 MILLION        FERTILITY 2
               PCT. TOTAL POP.

          0........5........10........15........20
 0 -  4 .         ::
 5 -  9 .         ::
10 - 14 .         ::
15 - 19 .         ::
20 - 24 .         ::
25 - 29 .         ::
30 - 34 .        ::
35 - 39 .        ::
40 - 44 .        ::
45 - 49 .        ::
50 - 54 .       ::
55 - 59 .        ::
60 - 64 .     ::
65 - 69 .    ::
70 - 74 .   ::
75+     .   ::
```

* Explain why the population continues to increase during the sixty years, even though women of child bearing age have an average of 2.0 children.
* Does the average age of the population decrease, stay about the same, or increase over the sixty years shown in the computer output? How would this affect the labor force?
* In 1970 what age range contains the largest percentage of the population? Trace this group of people over the sixty year span. Can you explain why the total population does not increase very much between 2020 and 2023?

A COMPUTER IN YOUR HOME?

The cheapest general-purpose factory-built computer costs about the same as a good color television set. It has a keyboard CRT terminal with a built-in microcomputer. Secondary storage uses a cassette tape recorder. Millions of people can afford to have such a computer in their homes, and many are buying them.

Other devices can be added to a small system, which of course, raises the price. A system with hardcopy printing, a disk memory system, and process control equipment attached will cost several thousand dollars. *What does one do with a home computer?* People who buy them are not yet aware of all the possible answers. Here are a few of them.

1. **Entertainment:** You have probably played various electronic video games like space wars or car races. The home computer can be used to play these games, as well as chess, checkers, and backgammon. It can also be used to generate art or music.
2. **Education:** The home computer can be used for computer assisted instruction. This can supplement the more traditional education for students, and can be used for adult education. The computer can also be used as an aid to solving problems in almost every field.
3. **Information retrieval**: A computerized address book can be used to print mailing labels. A compuerized recipe book could aid in meal planning. Some people are keeping tax records in their computer.
4. **Process control:** Devices such as a home's heating and lighting system can be computer controlled. Simpler examples include having a computer turn appliances such as TV, radio, or an electric coffee pot on or off at given times.

Suppose that you could have a complete computer system in your home. Make a list of ways you and the rest of your family could use it. Suggestion: think of uses in each of the four categories listed above. Think of uses by each member of your family. How would you use it during a weekend or during a vacation?

HOW COMPUTERS AFFECT PEOPLE

CHAPTER SEVEN

Computers are having a large impact upon this country and its people. Computers affect *you*, directly and indirectly. Test your knowledge about this area by answering each of the true-false questions given below.

T F (1) Most of the things computers do cannot be done in any other way.
T F (2) The telephone system makes extensive use of computers.
T F (3) The use of computers in medicine is growing rapidly.
T F (4) Automation, and use of computers, mean almost the same thing.
T F (5) Computers have wiped out many jobs, but they have also created many new jobs.
T F (6) Because computers are so expensive, they won't ever affect most people's jobs.
T F (7) Computers are essential to our space program (moon landing, satellites, etc.).
T F (8) In the future it is likely that computers will strongly affect what is taught in the schools, and will even help teach it.
T F (9) Computers can be used to invade your privacy, by helping to make information about you available.
T F (10) The U. S. government maintains a large computerized data bank that contains a large quantity of detailed information about every person in the U. S.

COMPUTERS AFFECT PEOPLE

Computers are having a large effect upon this country. For example, the entire space program depends upon computers. We could not have landed people upon the moon without computers. We could not have carried out the Mars landing and experiments without computers. Weather forecasting makes use of pictures from satellites. We now make extensive use of orbiting satellites for telephone and television communication. Of course you might argue that these things don't affect you very directly. So in this chapter we will look at some ways computers can, and maybe will, affect you directly.

GOODS AND SERVICES

Most of the things computers do can be done in other ways. So when a decision is made to use a computer it is usually because a computer can do the job better, quicker, cheaper, more reliably, etc. In the long run this affects you.

For example, consider the use of computers in the telephone system. They make the system more reliable. Connections are made faster, saving you time. Fewer operators, repair people, and billing clerks are needed. All of these things help keep the cost of telephone service down, giving us high quality telephone service at a reasonable price.

The banking industry provides another example. It is very convenient to write checks or use credit cards to pay for goods. But processing the checks and credit card sales slips is a big task. Without computers it would be much more expensive than it currently is.

We have discussed the use of computers in process control, and use of computerized robots on assembly lines. They reduce the cost of goods being manufactured and this reduced cost results in lower prices for you and/or in higher profits for the manufacturer.

When you read a newspaper, do you like it to contain up-to-date information? We have mentioned the role of computers in communication via telephone and satellite. Up-to-date information is available to the newspaper publisher, but how can it get printed quickly? Computerized typesetting is the answer. It is faster and cheaper than old style mechanical typesetting. Newspapers that use it can contain more up-to-date information.

The use of computers in medicine is growing rapidly. A computerized information retrieval system keeps track of all kinds of poisons, and what the best treatment is. Computers monitor patients in an intensive care unit of a hospital. Computers help diagnose a patient's disease. Computers are an essential tool of the medical researcher.

There are many tests that can be run on a patient visiting a doctor or hospital. A doctor can listen to your heart, and often can tell if there is something seriously wrong with it. A machine called an electrocardiograph is a big help. This machine records the electric current produced by the beating of a heart and produces a graph called an electrocardiogram. But not every doctor knows how to use this information about a heart, and it takes many years of training to be an expert in this field.

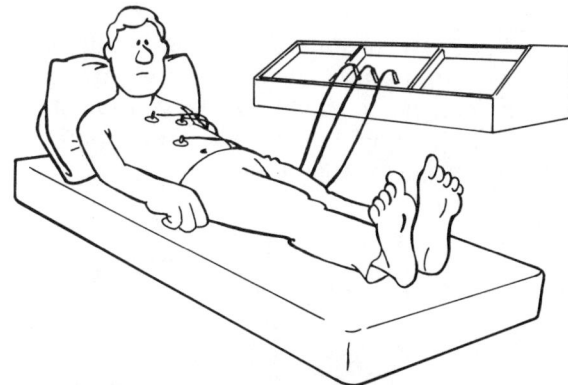

Now a computer can interpret an electrocardiogram rapidly and accurately, at a modest cost. This leads to better medical care, and helps hold down the cost of medical care.

Another example is blood testing. A nurse draws a blood sample, and puts it into a computerized machine. The machine automatically runs several dozen different tests on the blood, and prints out the results. Each year we see progress in making better machines for laboratory diagnostic use.

JOBS

You know what automation is, and how it affects people. Business and industry keep trying to increase productivity by using more and more machines to help each worker produce more. Automation existed a long time before computers and not all automation involves computers. Automobile assembly lines were highly automated back in the days when the Model A Ford was being built. But in recent years, computers have begun to have an impact.

Suppose you are an automobile assembly line worker making $7.50 per hour. Fringe benefits cost your employer another $2.50 per hour. So the total cost to your employer is $10.00 per hour. The job you do is to put the two left-side wheels on each car as the car moves past you.

Now your boss comes to you and says that a new $30,000 robot can do the same thing. It works for all makes and models of cars and is very reliable. The initial cost of $30,000 seems like a lot of money. But the robot can work 20 hours per day (a little time is needed for maintenance) and will last for many years. So the actual cost of this machine turns out to be just $3.00 per hour. *You are out of a job!*

Suppose you are the newest secretary working for a large law firm. The firm has many secretaries because there is so much routine typing to do. Much of your job is taking paragraphs from standard legal forms (wills and contracts) and retyping them to include the name of a client, the current date, etc.

Now computerized word processing machines are installed. One secretary can do the work that several used to do. Of course the machines are expensive, but they are cheap relative to the cost of secretaries. So you are out of a job!

Automation isn't the only place where computers are affecting people's jobs. Suppose that in the 1960s you worked in a company that made calculating machines. Your company produced electromechanical adding machines and other business machines. But then computer circuitry got cheaper and cheaper. By 1970 it was possible to build electronic calculators and business machines that were cheaper and better than your company's machines. Soon your company went bankrupt, everybody lost his job, and the company owners lost a lot of money.

For another example, consider electronic digital watches. One of the largest manufacturers of these watches is Texas Instruments. It also makes calculators, computers, and computer circuitry. But what about the companies that make mechanical watches? Some of them are going out of business.

It is important to understand that much automation does not depend upon computers. The problems of automation and the problems of changing technology were with us long before computers. But computers add to these problems. They make goods and services cheaper for those who have money. But people who lose their jobs cannot afford to buy the goods and services.

It is also important to understand that computers create jobs. A large number of people work as data entry clerks, computer operators, computer programmers, and so on. Many people have jobs designing, building, repairing, and selling computers. Because the use of computers is growing so rapidly, some of these job areas actually have a shortage of well qualified people. For example, many computer programming and computer analyst jobs require a four year college education. Current estimates are that there are about ten jobs of this sort available for each person graduating with a computer science degree.

EDUCATION

Computers are affecting both what is taught in schools, and how it is taught. We have mentioned how computers are used in running the business side of a school system. We also mentioned using computers to teach people.

Right now computers are just beginning to be used as an aid to instruction. In places where education is very expensive, computers are now common. For example, medical schools make extensive use of computer assisted instruction. Many big companies use computers to help train their employees. Computers are also being used in special education, such as with the deaf, blind, and with people with other physical or mental handicaps.

Still, most public schools don't currently use calculators and computers to help teach students. Up until now these machines have been too expensive, but that is changing very rapidly. A

simple example is provided by the pocket calculator. It is a useful aid in teaching math, and many elementary schools now have classroom sets of calculators. At the secondary school level, calculators are having an impact upon the teaching of science courses as well as math courses.

The use of computers as an aid to instruction will increase rapidly in the future. But equally important, computers have an effect upon what students are taught. What do students *need* to learn? They certainly don't want to spend a lot of time preparing for a certain career, only to see a computer take over that career. It doesn't make much sense to try to compete with a machine. So what should schools be doing to help students prepare for life in a computerized society?

There are two types of answers. First, teachers need to understand how computers affect the subject matter they teach. They can then teach something about computers when it is an important part of their subject matter. For example, consider the typing teacher in a high school. Some of the people taking the typing course just want to type well enough to do their own personal typing. Others are training to be secretaries. The future secretary will be faced with computerized word processing,

and will work in an office that uses computers for other purposes such as information retrieval. The typing teacher should know about these things, and the course should discuss these ideas.

The second type of answer requires joint work by students and the schools. Schools need to give courses about computers. They need to provide the opportunity for students to learn how to use computers. But that won't do any good unless students take the courses. Some aspects of learning to use a computer are easy. But some aspects are hard, and many students try to avoid hard courses. That is unfortunate, because these are the very students who are most likely to be automated out of a job sometime in the future.

BIG BROTHER IS WATCHING YOU

Many people are concerned about privacy. What information should the government keep about people? Who should have access to this information? How should this information be used?

Let's look at an example. The relation between cigarette smoking and lung cancer was discovered by a careful analysis of the medical records of a very large number of people. Much medical research depends upon having very detailed medical records of thousands of patients. This information is collected, and then stored in a computerized information retrieval system. The purpose is to help improve our knowledge of medicine.

But suppose that your records happen to be in this data bank, and you apply for a job. Suppose the company that is thinking about hiring you gains access to the computerized data bank. Maybe your medical record contains information you don't want the company to know, and because of this information, you don't get the job. This is an invasion of your privacy. It is a misuse of a computerized data bank.

Let's look at another example. Local, state, and federal governments have many data banks containing information about people. The local data banks contain registered voters, property tax payers, local police records, and so on. The state data banks contain information about state taxpayers, drivers licenses and motor vehicle registration, state police records, and state unemployment records. At the federal level there are the FBI files, military service files, social security files, and internal revenue files.

From time to time people propose that all of these files be combined. They say it would be more efficient. Much duplication could be avoided. It would help the police and FBI. Maybe a "wanted" person is paying income tax, or has registered a motor vehicle.

But such a massive data bank could lead to an invasion of privacy. Various parts of the government could find out things about you that they have no right to know. Various people who had access to the data bank could easily use it for unauthorized purposes. For reasons such as this, federal lawmakers have continually defeated proposals for such a national data bank.

But we are rapidly moving in this direction by other means. Perhaps you have read about electonic funds transfer (EFT). The idea is simple enough. You go into a store and buy something using a credit card. The store has a machine that can read your name and account number off the card, and telephone it to the bank's computer. The bank's computer immediately takes the money for the purchase out of your account and puts it in the store's account.

Now let's combine EFT with the UPC (universal product code) in a grocery store. You enter a grocery store at 8:45 in the evening. You purchase some wine, beer, cigarettes, peanuts, and candy, paying for them with your EFT credit card. The store's computer then has a record of your name, the time, the date, and exactly what items you bought.

Suppose that this information was combined with the airline reservation system information. Suppose that the airline system just happened to show that your spouse was out of town at that time. We now have all the ingredients for blackmail! The computer data suggests you are having a late evening party while your spouse is out of town!

There are other very large data banks that can be used for such purposes. One example is credit bureau files. When a person tries to buy something on credit, the store is interested in how good a credit risk the person represents. Companies that do credit investigation keep large computerized files on all the information they obtain about people. They add to this file by keeping track of police records, newspaper articles, and court records. They also carry out investigations by asking your neighbors about you.

In the past each credit bureau was small and contained information about people in a single town or small part of a state. But several of these companies are now very large with data banks that contain information about many millions of people.

This information can be accessed using computer terminals. Its misuse can be an invasion of your privacy.

At one time you did not even have the legal right to find out what information a credit bureau was keeping on you or to correct errors in it. Sometimes a person would apply for credit, and be turned down for reasons that were not made clear. Often there was no real reason—merely errors in the credit bureau's files. There was little a person could do about this before 1970. In that year the federal government passed a law that allows people to see what is in their credit bureau files, and allows them to correct errors.

Computerized data banks are a serious threat to people's privacy. They can be used to obtain detailed information about you, your job, how you spend your money, your travels, etc. But laws can be developed to help prevent this. It is not easy to make good laws of this sort. The laws must allow businesses and government to continue to function well. But the laws must protect you against unreasonable invasion of privacy.

COMPUTER CAREERS

There are a large number of people who have computer-related jobs. Some people build, repair, or sell computers. Others work as data entry clerks or computer operators, while still others work as computer programmers, systems analysts, or managers of computer installations. And, of course, many people interact with computers every day in their jobs, such as selling airline tickets, handling motel reservations, or clerking in a store.

In the early history of the computer industry most people were trained on the job. There was a great shortage of people

who had received high school or college training for working with computers. But in recent years this has changed. Now there are many high school and community college programs that train computer operators and technicians. There are many community college, college, and university programs that train computer programmers and systems analysts. Almost all of these positions now require formal academic training plus continued on-the-job training and experience.

The type of training one needs for a computer-related job depends upon the particular job. Computer repair people must have specialized training in electronics repair work. Manual dexterity and good intelligence are needed. Many people receive this type of training via military service schools.

Data entry positions generally require good typing skills. The data entry clerk must learn to deal with a variety of data entry devices, have good speed, and good accuracy. Pay scales tend to be comparable to secretarial pay scales.

Computer programmers and system analysts need to be good at solving problems and at learning new things. Often they need to know both the computer field and the field in which they are applying computers. A college degree involving both business courses and computers is desirable for people wanting to work in business data processing.

Computing is a rapidly growing industry. Current estimates are that the number of jobs in the industry is growing at the rate of 10% per year. If this continues for a few more years, which seems likely, then computing will become one of the largest segments of our economy and job market.

CONCLUSIONS

As time goes on, computers will have a bigger and bigger impact upon people. This is bound to occur, because computers are versatile and useful machines. They are getting cheaper. And people are gaining more knowledge on how to use computers.

How computers affect you in the future will depend quite a lot upon you. You can try to learn more about computers. You can help to encourage the passage of laws to guard your privacy. You can study for a career that will not be wiped out by computers. If you do these things, you will be able to cope with computers. If you don't, who knows what will happen?

HOW'S YOUR MEMORY?

What are the names of these pieces of computer equipment? Choose from the list below.

microcomputer with CRT
keypunch machine
line printer
tape drive
UPC reader

large computer system
plotter
disk drive
optical mark reader (scanner)
keyboard terminal (hard copy)

WHAT DID THE HOME COMPUTER SAY TO ITS NEW OWNER?

To find out, fill in the letter of the best response.

___ 1. The person who writes instructions that tell the computer how to handle information is the (a) programmer (b) computer operator (c) technician (d) data entry clerk
___ 2. A data entry clerk (a) supervises the computer operations (b) writes the instructions to the computer (c) transcribes the instructions into computer readable form
___ 3. Computer operators will (d) install and maintain equipment (e) supervise machine operations (f) transcribe material onto cards or tape.
___ 4. Compared to other people in the computer field, key punch operators earn a relatively (d) low salary (e) medium salary (f) high salary
___ 5. The person who installs and maintains equipment is called a (k) field engineer or computer technician (l) computer operator (m) systems analyst
___ 6. The person who develops methods of using the computer to solve problems is the (k) computer operator (l) manager (m) systems analyst
___ 7. A 4-year college degree would generally be required for a person to become a (m) data entry clerk (n) computer operator (o) systems analyst
___ 8. The person who classifies, catalogs and maintains reference material used for processing is called the (n) computer operator (o) systems analyst (p) documents librarian
___ 9. The person earning the highest salary, relative to the others given, is the (r) programmer (s) systems analyst (t) computer operator
___ 10. Data entry is a job that (r) requires programming knowledge (s) requires a 4-year college degree (t) requires little knowledge about the computer
___ 11. A computer programmer needs to be able to (r) think logically, and like detailed work (s) type data into the computer quickly (t) operate all the different types of computer equipment

___12. The person who repairs computers and does preventive maintenance is the (u) technician (v) systems analyst (w) salesperson

___13. The number of computer related jobs is (x) decreasing (y) increasing (z) remaining about the same

Use your responses to find the computer's question.

$$\overline{\underset{4}{}\,\underset{7}{}}\quad \overline{\underset{13}{}\,\underset{7}{}\,\underset{12}{}}\quad \overline{\underset{9}{}\,\underset{8}{}\,\underset{3}{}\,\underset{1}{}\,\underset{5}{}}$$

$$\overline{\underset{2}{}\,\underset{7}{}\,\underset{6}{}\,\underset{8}{}\,\underset{12}{}\,\underset{10}{}\,\underset{3}{}\,\underset{11}{}\,\underset{3}{}\,\underset{1}{}\,\underset{9}{}\,\underset{3}{}}\quad ?$$

THOUGHT QUESTIONS

Make a list of all the places where there are records containing detailed information about you (school records, medical records, etc.). What is in these records? Who has access to these records? Would you like it if all your friends (and enemies) had easy access to all of these records? Discuss why or why not.

It is sometimes suggested that we are becoming a "cashless" society. More and more goods and services are paid for by check or credit card. What are the obstacles to completely stopping the use of cash? What would the effects be? Would you like this to happen? Discuss this situation and the likelihood that it will occur in the next 20 years.

HAVE YOU READ?

These are a few of the many science fiction stories written about computers. The writers of science fiction predict the future by using scientific information and their imaginations. Some writers have been very accurate in their predictions. Arthur C. Clarke is especially noted for this, with his stories about life on the moon, space platforms and computers.

But some writers show a lack of understanding even of current technology, much less of what it may come to be. So it is fun to read science fiction stories (or watch s-f films) and try to decide if the author understands technology.

IF YOU ARE INTERESTED...

* Here are some popular s-f stories about computers. In reading any of them, decide if the author's prediction could someday be true.

"The Nine Billion Names of God"
"The Feeling of Power"
The Electronic Olympics
The City and the Stars

* Look in your library for s-f books or short stories by these authors. How accurate could they be?

Asimov
Bova
Bradbury
Clark
Heinlein

* What prediction did Jules Verne or H. G. Wells make that actually came true many years later?

* Write your own science fiction story or play with computers in it. Use your knowledge and imagination, even possibly a friend, to help get started. Think about what computers *can do*: help people recover in a hospital, elect public officials or win a war, commit crimes, and destroy people.

HAVE YOU READ?

THE ELECTRONIC OLYMPICS

In this book a computer called PED-70 becomes the first "official judge" at the Olympic events. A sports photographer covers the world Olympics and finds he dislikes the idea of mechanical sports and "programmed" athletes.

You may have heard or read about problems with the judging at Olympic events in the past. Judges from one country may give an athlete bad marks and in turn see their own athletes face poor scores from a different country.

What is the major advantage of computerized judging?

What sports would be easy to judge with the help of a computer *now*?

What are some problems that could occur with computerized judging?

Are there any gymnastic events that you think a computer could judge?

Write a short story, poem or play about a big athletic event that you organize in the year 2000.

"HARDCASTLE"

In this short story a couple rents a fully automated house. They have to get used to a computer in the basement, many servomechanisms, a robot-controlled indoor environmental system, an electronic entertainment center with a wall-sized TV screen and a memory bank of 3000 classic films, and finally the house's ability to make "conversation" with them.

What kinds of things in *your* house would you like to have computerized? Decide if that would be practical in the next 5 years, the next 20 years.

COMPUTERS AND SOCIETY

Many people have accepted the idea of change in our society and thus easily adapt to a computerized future. Others react negatively to computers and find the use of machines threatening. The pattern for change is set. Decreasing the use of computers is simply not one of our choices. So it is important that people understand the computer as a beneficial tool with some disadvantages.

1984 and *Brave New World* made people aware of the possibility of a mechanized future. Because of this awareness, it may be less likely to happen. However, many people are extremely distrustful of technology as a result.

Here are some additional resources about computers and society, both present and future. Most of the articles or books are written at an adult level.

Archer, Marcin, "Fictional Computers and Their Themes," *Computers and Automation*, Dec. 1962.

"Computers in Science Fiction—II," *Computers and Automation*, Nov. 1973.

Baer, Robert M., *The Digital Villain*, 1972, Reading, MA, Addison Wesley.

Bertran, Raphael, *The Thinking Computer: Mind Inside Matter*, 1976, San Francisco, CA, W. H. Freeman Press.

Feigenbaum, Edward A., and Feldman, Julian (editors), *Computers and Thought*, 1963, New York, NY, McGraw-Hill Book Co.

Mowskowitz, Abbe, *Inside Information: Computers in Fiction*, 1977, Reading, MA: Addison Wesley.

Spencer, Donald, *Computers in Action: How Computers Work*, 1974, Rochelle Park, NJ, Hayden Book Co., Inc.

Computers in Society: The Wheres, Whys and Hows of Computer Use, 1974, Rochelle Park, NJ, Hayden Book Co., Inc.

Van Tassel, Dennie L., *The Compleat Computer*, 1976, Chicago, Science Research Associates.

Weizenbaum, Joseph, *Computer Power and Human Reason: From Judgment to Calculation*, 1976, San Francisco, CA, W. H. Freeman.

Winkless, Nels, and Browning, Iben, *Robots on Your Doorstep*, 1978, Portland, OR, Robotics Press

HAVE YOU READ?
SCIENCE FICTION

BOOKS

Ben Bova, *Escape*   *The Multiple Man*

Robert Heinlein, *The Moon is a Harsh Mistress*

Arthur C. Clarke, *The Nine Billion Names of God*
  Contains a short story by the same name and also "The Sentinal," which inspired the film 2001: A Space Odyssey.

  The City and the Stars

Hal Higdon, *The Electronic Olympics*

Ira Levin, *This Perfect Day*

SHORT STORIES

Isaac Asimov, "Franchise"
  A fully computerized election.

  "The Feeling of Power"
  About the return of brain power—or the possibility of man replacing computers.

  "The Pacifist"
  About a computer that works with math problems but mutinies if given a military problem.

  "The Thinking Machine"
  The author explains the difference between a human brain and the computer.

Ray Bradbury, "There Will Come Soft Rains"
  Another automated house in future society.

Frederic Brown, "The Answer"
  A computer answers the question about the existence of God.

Ron Goulart, "Hardcastle"
  Couple try to live in a computerized house.

Bruce Karwin, "Form 5640: Report of a Malfunction"
  A computer terminal replaces a welfare worker and breaks down.

Stanislaw Lem, "The Computer That Fought a Dragon"
  Creation of a cyberdragon.

Louis B. Salomon, "Univac to Univac"
　Machines talk to each other about humans.

Kurt Vonnegut, "Epicac"
　A computer writes love poems and eventually falls in love.

CHAPTER EIGHT

WHAT ELSE IS THERE TO KNOW?

This chapter gives you more information about the field of computers. Try these questions and check your answers to see how much more there is to know.

T F (1) You must know a lot about computers before you can use them.
T F (2) Many thousands of people have bought computers for use in their homes.
T F (3) A computer library is a special library where you can only check out books about computers.
T F (4) The best computers can now carry on a conversation in English, much like one sees robots doing on TV programs.
T F (5) You can run programs without knowing how to write them.
T F (6) If a computer can solve a certain type of math problem, then the computer is undoubtedly the best way to solve the problem.
T F (7) Computer programmers must be good at solving complicated problems.
T F (8) Even though there are hundreds of computer programs available, it might be necessary to write your own in order to solve a problem.
T F (9) It is easy for a computer to translate the English language into a foreign language.
T F (10) Artificial intelligence has to do with how smart a computer can be.

By now you may think that you know just about all there is to know about computers. Certainly you know more than you did when you began reading this book, but there is still a lot more to learn. Some people spend their entire lives studying about computers. There are thousands of books and journals about computers. This chapter will give you information on some other things you might want to learn.

COMPUTER LITERACY

A computer is a tool that can be used to help solve many different kinds of problems, It is an aid to *doing* something. A computer is a machine that millions of people *use* on a daily basis.

But this book wasn't designed to teach you how to do something. It doesn't teach you how to use a computer. It doesn't show you any of the details on how a computer can help solve a business, mathematics, or science problem.

The goal of this book is to increase your level of computer literacy. We want you to know more about what computers can do, and what they cannot do. We want you to understand how computers affect society, and you. We want you to be aware of the problems computers create for our educational system, government, and you.

If you have studied and thought about the material in previous chapters you are now more computer literate. Also, you have built a foundation for gaining more knowledge about computers. You have learned some of the main ideas and vocabulary.

Now when you read, or watch television, you will pay more attention to articles or programs that mention computers. You will be able to tell if a TV program is giving computers powers that they do not have. Now when you, or your children, take a course you will understand that the teacher should be including information on how computers are used to help solve problems in that field. Maybe you will ask the teacher how computers have affected that field. If you do these things your knowledge about computers will continue to grow.

Still, there is much you cannot learn about computers in this way. Three general areas that require studying and hard work are presented in the next three sections. If you are serious about learning more about computers, these are the things you will need to learn.

What Else is There to Know?

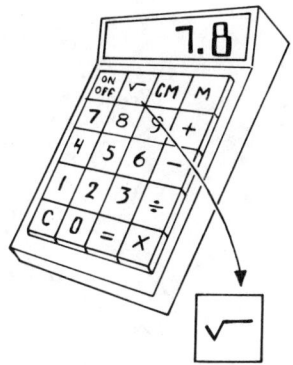

USING COMPUTERS

One can use a computer without knowing much about them. We can see this by looking at a calculator example. Suppose you wanted to know the square root of 78.49, and you had a calculator with a square root key. You would merely key in 78.49 and depress the square root key. The calculator would then display the answer. The program to compute square root is in the calculator's memory. The calculator automatically follows this program when you depress the square root key.

So it is with computers. There are thousands of programs that have been written, and are available for people to use. A collection of these programs is called a *computer library*, and using one is often quite easy.

The steps involved in using a library program to solve a problem are as follows:

1. Understand the problem.
2. Decide if a computer can help solve the problem. Assuming it can:
3. Find a computer library program designed to solve the problem. Assuming you can find one:
4. Read about how to prepare the data so the program can process it.
5. Prepare the data.
6. Use the computer program to process the data.
7. Read, understand, and use the results produced by the computer.

In the above list the word "problem" refers to a large task whose solution is more suited to a machine than to a person working by hand. For example, suppose you were interested in finding out whether the left handed students get better grades than the right handed students. Obviously not every left handed

student gets better grades than every right handed student. So what you probably want to know about is their average grades.

But perhaps left handed students don't take the same courses as right handed students. The more one thinks about this problem, the harder it becomes. Computer programs exist that can do the necessary statistical analysis. But *you* must figure out what statistical analysis to perform. *You* must gather the data and put it into machine readable form. *You* must figure out the meaning of the computer's output that results from doing the statistical analysis.

Let's look once more at the seven steps for using a library program. Steps 1 and 7 require that you understand the problem, and understand the meaning of a solution to the problem, which requires that you understand the subject area connected with the problem. The computer is no substitute for learning "traditional" subject matter. If you don't know something about statistical analysis then you cannot hope to solve the left versus right handedness problem.

Step 2 requires you to decide if a computer is a useful aid. This requires knowledge of computers and of the types of steps needed to solve the problem. Thus you have to have some insight

into the types of processes required to solve the problem, although you don't need to know all of the details.

Step 3 requires searching computer libraries. This requires that one be able to read computer library materials, and understand descriptions of what various programs can do. These

```
LIB
   ACT        ELECT
      BAGELS
   BIOSIN     HAIKU
      STR*1
              POLUT
```

descriptions are often quite technical. They use the vocabulary of both the computer field and of the problem subject matter field.

Steps 4 and 5 involve data preparation. This is a major part of solving many problems. The data must be collected and put into computer readable form. Details of the allowable data form are included in the computer library materials.

Step 6 involves actually using the computer. Sometimes it takes only a few minutes of instruction and practice to learn to do this. But some computer library programs are so complicated that it takes weeks of study and practice to learn how to use them. Some people make a living helping other people to use computer library programs.

As you can see, it is not necessary to know how to write computer programs in order to use a computer. The great majority of all computer usage involves using library programs. Quite often people using the programs did not help write them,

and do not know how to write programs. But it is clear that some people need to know how to write computer programs.

COMPUTER PROGRAMMING

There are several reasons why you might want to learn how to write computer programs:

1. To increase your level of computer literacy.
2. To improve your ability to decide whether a computer will be a useful aid in solving a particular problem.
3. To write programs to solve problems that cannot be solved using programs in the library.
4. Because it is fun.

We will discuss each of these briefly.

A computer literacy course covers materials like those in this book. Such a course often includes considerable "hands-on" experience in using a computer. That experience involves using library programs, and may also involve learning to write simple programs. Many educational experts argue that people must have some practice in writing programs if they are to be computer literate.

It is often difficult to decide if a computer will be a useful aid in helping to solve a problem. What at first glance appears to be a computer problem might better be solved by use of a calculator or by use of math tables. It can require considerable knowledge about computers in order to make a correct decision. In the simple cases the necessary programs have probably been written and are in a program library. In the hard cases the programs have not been written. How difficult will it be to write the necessary programs? What will it cost? Questions like this can only be answered by a person who knows a lot about computer programming.

Although a computer library may contain hundreds or even thousands of programs, most problems do not fit one of these programs. The computer library only contains programs for problems that arise over and over again. Thus, if you are doing anything new, or any type of original research, you are apt to run into problems that cannot be solved using the library programs. This is a good reason for people to learn how to write programs.

For many people writing computer programs is fun. It can be a challenging intellectual task. One has the reward of developing something new and being in charge of the machine. For these

and many other reasons, computers are becoming a popular commercial item for the home. Many people own their own computers. A few years ago these were people who bought computer kits and assembled them. Now one can buy many different brands of fully assembled factory built computers. These microcomputers cost about the same as color television sets. Many people enjoy writing programs, developing computer games, and finding new uses for their computers.

It is very easy to learn how to write simple computer programs which solve simple problems. But it is not easy to learn how to write complex computer programs to solve difficult problems. There are two reasons for this. First, there is the difficulty of writing a complex program. This requires considerable training, experience, and knowledge of computer science. (See the next section, on computer science.) Second, it requires

knowledge on how to solve difficult problems. If you cannot solve difficult problems without a computer, then you won't be any better at it using a computer.

COMPUTER SCIENCE

There are many parts of computer science that have been mentioned in this book. For example, computer literacy, computer simulation, computer graphics, information retrieval, process control, and computer programming are all parts of computer science. Computer science includes the study of all aspects of building and using computers. We will discuss a few more aspects in this section.

What Else is There to Know? 119

Electrical engineers are interested in designing computer circuitry and building computers. Thus every engineering college offers some courses that have to do with the design of computer circuitry. Indeed, the entire engineering profession is very concerned with computers. Almost all engineers are required to learn how to program and use a computer while they are in college. Many engineering colleges offer a complete program of study leading to a college degree in computer science.

Earlier in this book we mentioned computer programming languages such as BASIC, COBOL, and PASCAL. Computer scientists study the existing programming languages and they design new languages. They try to develop languages that will be easier to learn and easier to use for solving hard problems. Computer scientists are interested in the theory of programming languages and in the theory of solving problems by computer. Much of their research work is highly mathematical in nature.

Up to this point we have completely ignored one of the most interesting and important parts of computer science. It is called artificial intelligence (AI). AI has to do with the question of how "smart" a computer can be. Suppose you didn't know how to do long division. If you saw a calculator doing long division you would be impressed. You would think the machine was pretty smart.

So it is with computers. Computers have been programmed to play games such as checkers and chess. They can play these games quite well, but does this mean that computers are smart? Computers solve many kinds of problems that are too difficult for people to do by hand. Just to understand what problem is being solved may well take a college education in some cases.

It really doesn't make much difference whether or not we call this being smart. What is important is that the ideas used to

make a computer play good checkers can also make a computer solve other problems. Medical diagnostic problems are quite a bit like checker and chess problems. So as people learn to write "smarter" programs, they learn to write programs that can do *better* medical diagnostic work.

One problem currently of interest to people studying artificial intelligence is language and speech. Can we develop computer programs that can understand spoken English? Can we develop programs that can translate from English into another language? Can we develop programs that can carry on a conversation with a person, and help the person to solve problems? These are very difficult problems. Some progress has occurred, but so far none of these problems has been completely solved.

It is easy to see why AI is an interesting and difficult part of computer science. The problems it tries to solve are very difficult and the implications of research in AI are very important. Computers can already do some "thinking type" things better than people. Progress in AI will add more things to this list. Will

What Else is There to Know?

computers someday be smarter than people? It is clear that we are a long, long way from being there, but who can see the future? It could well be that some day computers will be better than people in solving many kinds of problems.

WHAT SHOULD YOU DO?

If you are a student, then you face the decision of what courses to take. You know that some courses are easy, and some are hard. It is possible to take mostly easy courses and to "get by."

If that is your goal, you probably won't want to learn much more about computers. Computer programming is not an easy subject. Learning to use a computer to help solve difficult problems is not easy. The various topics that make up computer science are not easy.

But suppose you are interested in computer science. Then you should plan to go to college. There you can study computer science, or computers in business, or many other uses of computers. Meanwhile, you should take courses that will prepare you for this type of college career. That means, take the hard courses. Develop good reading and writing skills. Learn mathematics. Study the application areas, such as business, the social sciences, and the sciences.

At the same time you can continue to learn more about computers. You will want to begin reading books and magazines about computers. You will want to find out more about how computers are being used. You will want to get to know other people who are interested in computers. Get started now!

MACHINE MATCH-UP

Match the letters of the words in column B with their descriptions in column A. Not all words will be used.

Column A
- ___ 1. A TV-like display screen
- ___ 2. Magnetic-type primary storage
- ___ 3. The instructions to a computer
- ___ 4. The information that comes out of a computer on devices like line printers and plotters.
- ___ 5. A computer that stores and processes information by using numbers.
- ___ 6. A system where many people use the computer at the same time.
- ___ 7. The part of a computer that does the mathematics of a problem.
- ___ 8. Primary and secondary storage
- ___ 9. A computer that works by using continuously varying quantities
- ___10. A keyboard device like a typewriter hooked up to a computer by wires.
- ___11. A machine used for punching holes in cards.

Column B
A. memory
B. magnetic disk
C. terminal
D. plotter
E. digital computer
F. magnetic drum
G. optical scanner
H. binary symbols
I. keypunch
J. statement
K. chip
L. core
M. arithmetic unit
N. paper-tape
O. time-sharing
P. cathode ray tube
Q. magnetic tape
R. program
S. control unit
T. output
U. analog computer

Now, place each letter used in a box below, under the corresponding number. THEN, CONSIDER YOURSELF . . . . .

10	6	7	1	9	4	5	3		2	11	4	5	3	8	4	5	
																	!

What Else is There to Know?

INTELLIGENT COMPUTER

Suppose that some people came to you and said they had just finished building an intelligent computer. Would you believe them? How can one tell if a computer is intelligent? Devise a test for the computer to take.

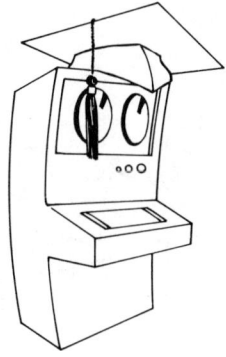

Do you think that computer literacy can be measured by a 10 question true-false test? Make up a 10 question literacy test. Each question should test a very important aspect of computer literacy. Then try out the test on at least five people who have not read this book. If they make mistakes, explain to them why their answers are not correct.

Computers can play checkers and chess quite well because humans have written detailed computer programs that tell the computers how to figure out good moves. Select a simple game, such as tic-tac-toe. Can you write down a precise set of directions that tell a person how to play the game quite well? Try it. Your goal is to write a set of directions that is so good that the person following them will never lose.

COMPUTER CAREERS

The use of keypunch machines to prepare data for input to a computer is gradually declining. Other forms of data entry, such as the use of key to tape, key to disk, and optical character recognition are gradually replacing the use of punched cards. However, about 500,000 keypunch machines have been manufactured in the United States.

Check the help wanted ads in several newspapers, including at least one newspaper from a large city. See how many jobs you can find for keypunch operators and for other data entry positions. Also look for ads for other positions in the computer field, such as computer programmer and system analyst.

Make a notebook of ads from computer-related jobs, and of other information related to computer careers. An excellent source of ads is the *COMPUTERWORLD* weekly newspaper.

HAVE YOU READ?

THE COMPUTER PROPHETS

This book, by Jerry Rosenberg, contains very interesting biographies of men who developed computing devices. There's a lot of fascinating information in the life stories, struggles and achievements of the men in this book:

What Else is There to Know?

Blaise Pascal
J. Presper Eckert
Herman Hollerith
Charles Babbage
Alan M. Turing
Thomas J. Watson
Dorr E. Felt

William S. Burroughs
Gottfried Wilhelm Leibnitz
John von Neumann
Howard Aiken
George Barnard Grant
Robert M. Fano
John W. Mauchly

ADDITIONAL RESOURCES

RESOURCE BOOKS

Introductory (intermediate grade levels)

Computers, Melvin Burger, Coward McCann Geoghegan, Inc., New York, 1972.
Computers, Jane Jonas Srivastava, Thomas Y. Crowell Co., New York, 1972.
My Friend the Computer, Jean Rice, T. S. Denison and Company, Inc., Minneapolis, Minnesota, 1976.
What is a Computer?, Marion Ball, Houghton-Mifflin, Boston, 1972.
Computers: Tools for Today, Claude J. DeRossi, Children's Press, Chicago, Illinois, 1972.
The Story of Computers, Donald Spencer, Abacus Computer Corporation, Ormond Beach, Florida, 1975.

Secondary (middle school through senior high grades)

Computers, Fred Steinberg, Franklin Watts, Inc., New York, 1969.
Computers and Automation, John A. Brown, Arco Publishing Co., New York, 1968.
The Computer Revolution, Nigel Hawkes, E. P. Dutton, New York, 1968.
Computer Poems, Collected by Richard W. Bailey, Potagannissing Press, Ann Arbor, Michigan.

Electric Media, Les Brown and Simon Marks, Harcourt Brace Jovanovich, New York, NY 10017.

Peanut Butter and Jelly Guide to Computers, Jerry Willis, dilithium Press, Portland, OR, 1978.

Dictionaries

Computer Glossary for Students and Teachers, L. C. Schmaly and C. J. Sippl, Funk & Wagnalls, New York, 1972.

Home Computers: A Beginner's Glossary and Guide, Merl Miller and Charles Sippl, dilithium Press, Portland, OR, 1978

The Laymen's Dictionary of Computer Technology, Norman and Eileen Sondak, Hawthorn Books Inc., New York, 1973

COMPUTER FILMS

The following films are listed to provide more information to students and for a source of discussion in class.

Art from Computers, 7-A, 8 minutes, Control Data Corporation
  Computer graphics and mathematics combine to produce artistic designs.
A Better World, 10-A, 8 minutes, Modern Talking Picture
  The influence of computers is described in a fast montage of applications.
A Computer Glossary, 10-A, 10 minutes, Photo and Sound
  Defines basic terms with animation and explains some of the complex micro-circuitry of a computer.
The Computer, 2-6, 11 minutes.
  Introductory information about what kind of machine the computer is.
The Computer Revolution, 7-A, 23 minutes, Modern Talking Pictures
  General introduction to computers, emphasizes present uses and potential in the future.
Computers, 4-9, 11 minutes, AIMS
  Describes major components of a computer and the binary system.
Future Shock, 9-A, 42 minutes, McGraw-Hill
  Based on Alvin Toffler's book, the film explores events happening *now*.

Additional Resources

The Information Machine, 7-A, 11 minutes, Modern Talking Pictures
Animated account of the development of the electronic computer.

Introduction to Digital Computers, 7-A, 24 minutes, Univac Division.
Animation of five basic computer parts as well as literary information.

Man and Computer . . . A Perspective, 10-A, 20 minutes, Modern Talking Pictures.
Explains basic elements in data processing with live action and animation.

Marvelous Calculator, 10-A, 19 minutes, Modern Talking Pictures.
History of the computer is shown from earliest known origin to present day.

Medical Electronics, 30 minutes, Modern Talking Pictures
Computer as it relates to future medicine.

Thinking?? Machine, 7-A, 19 minutes, BELT
Animated comparison of computational processes of computer to the human brain.

2001, 7-A, 25 minutes, Rarigs, Inc.
The world of tomorrow, narrated by Walter Cronkite, shows a computerized home.

You and the Computer, 7-A, 9 minutes, GENE
Shows the computer in basic business functions.

Write to these sources for current catalogs that describe films about computers or automation. Most of them are free.

Association—Sterling Films
866 Third Avenue
New York, NY 10022
(ask for a regional catalog)

Bell Telephone Laboratories
(contact your local Bell office)

Photo and Sound
1205 North 45th Street
Seattle, Washington 98103

Modern Talking Picture Service
1205 North 45th Street
Seattle, Washington 98103
(source for IBM films)
(ask for regional catalog)

National Aeronautics and Space Administration
National Audio Visual Center (GSA)
Washington, D. C. 20409

Contemporary/McGraw Hill Films*
Film Rental Library
McGraw Hill Book Company
P. O. Box 590
Heightstown, NJ 08520

Control Data Corporation
8100 South 34th Avenue
Minneapolis, Minnesota 55420

Dept. of Transportation
Federal Aviation Administration
Washington, D. C.

Document Associates, Inc.
573 Church Street
Toronto 285, Ontario, Canada

General Dynamics
Electronics Division
5011 Kearney Villa Road
San Diego, CA 92123

Pyramid Films*
Box 1048
Santa Monica, CA 90406

Rarigs, Inc.
200 West Mercer
Seattle, Washington

Univac Division
Sperry Rand Corporation Film
  Library
P. O. Box 500
Blue Bell, PA 19422

*Rental fee

INFORMATION, PLEASE

Here are some resources for free material. Single copies of pamphlets are sent if named and asked for on school stationery.

Computers, by William R. Corliss, U. S. Atomic Energy Commission, Office of Information Services, P. O. Box 62, Oak Ridge, Tennessee 37830, 1973

Facts on Computer Careers, American Federation of Information Processing Societies, Communications Dept., 1815 North Lynn St., Suite 800, Arlington, VA 22209.

Mighty New Servant to the Mind of Man, Sperry Rand Corporation, Univac Division, 1290 Avenue of the Americas, New York, New York, 10019, 1964

The Computer Age, More About Computers, International Business Machines Corporation, Old Orchard Road, Armonk, New York, 10504, 1966

Additional Resources

These are companies that might have material available at little or no cost:

American Telephone and Telegraph Co., 195 Broadway, New York, NY 10007
Hewlett Packard Co., 1501 Page Mill Road, Palo Alto, CA, 94304
Texas Instruments Inc., P. O. Box 1444, Houston, Texas, Digital Systems Division
Honeywell, Inc., Honeywell Plaza, Minneapolis, Minnesota 55408
Rockwell International Corp.,600 Grant St.,Pittsburgh PA 15219
Bell Industries, 1880 Century Park E., Los Angeles, CA 90067
Lockheed Missiles and Space Co., Inc., P. O. Box 504, Sunnyvale, CA
Wang Laboratories, 826 North Street, Tewksburg, MA 01876
Burroughs Corp., Computer Systems Group, Burroughs Place, Detroit, Michigan, 48232
Westinghouse Electric Corp., Computer and Instrumentations Division, 200 Beta Drive, Pittsburgh, PA, 15222
IBM Corporate Headquarters, Old Orchard Road, Armonk, NY 10504

COMPUTERS AND MUSIC

Articles

Hiller, Lejaren A. Jr., "Computer Music," *Scientific American*, Vol. 201 (December, 1959), pp. 109-120.
Ladner, Robert Jr., "Computer Analysis of Music Forms," *Music Journal*, Vol. 26 (October, 1968), pp. 33, 58.
Mathews, M. J.; Moore, F. R.; and Risset, J. C., "Computers and Future Music," *Science*, Vol. 183, No. 4122 (January 25, 1974), pp. 263-268.
Seay, Albert, "What is Electronic Music?" *Music Journal*, Vol. 21 (March, 1963), pp. 26, 60-61.

Films

"Art from Computers," NBC Educational Enterprises, Canada, 1971. 10 min.

"Discovering Electronic Music," Bailey Film Association, 1970. 23 min.
"New Sounds in Music," Churchill Films, 1969. 22 min.
"Pretty Lady and the Electronic Musicians," Xerox, 1972. 14 min.

Records

Computer Music, from the University of Illinois, Hiller/Isaacson/Baker, Helioda (H/HS 25053). Metro-Goldwyn-Mayer, 1350 Avenue of the Americas, New York, NY 10019.
  Side 1: Illiac Suite for String Quartet
  Side 2: Computer Cantata

Computer Music from the Computer Center of Columbia and Princeton Universities, Randall/Vercoe/Dodge, Nonesuch Records (H-71245), 15 Columbia Circle, New York, NY 10023

Music From Mathematics played by the IBM 7090 Computer and Digital to Sound Transducer, Decca Records (DL 9103)

Oxygene played on four synthesizers and a rhythm computer by Jean-Michel Jarre, Polydor Inc., New York. Original recording by Disques Motors—France

COMPUTER LITERACY EXAM

Circle the *best* response of the four choices listed to complete each statement.

1. What is computer literacy? Is it:
   a. The ability to write computer programs?
   b. Knowing what a computer can and cannot do, how computers are used, and how they may change our lives?
   c. Knowing computer-related vocabulary, so you can read, write, and talk about computers?
   d. Understanding how to build a computer?
2. The first general purpose electronic digital computer became operational:
   a. Shortly after Ben Franklin performed his famous experiment using a kite and lightening.
   b. Shortly after the invention of the telephone.
   c. About the time the first television set was built.
   d. Shortly after the end of World War II.
3. A task quite suited to a computer is:
   a. To print out "personalized" form letters for advertising purposes.
   b. To take off, pilot, and land a small plane flying from San Francisco to Los Angeles.
   c. To analyze an X-ray and recommend a course of treatment for any diseases it detects.
   d. To take over most functions currently performed by teachers.

4. A good way to think about computers is:
   a. It is impossible for a computer to tell a lie.
   b. Computers are built and programmed by people and these people should be responsible for what computers do.
   c. Anything a human can do a computer can do better.
   d. Any problem that can be solved by a computer should be, since a computer cannot make a mistake.
5. A *good* definition of a computer is:
   a. An electronic automated device that can solve problems involving words and numbers.
   b. A superspeed pocket calculator.
   c. A machine that uses binary numbers to do math problems.
   d. Any machine that can add, subtract, multiply, and divide numbers.
6. When we say a computer "understands" an instruction we mean:
   a. The computer can execute (carry out) that instruction.
   b. The computer can explain the meaning of that instruction.
   c. The computer's keyboard has a key corresponding to the instruction.
   d. It can print out a definition of the instruction.
7. A magnetic disk pack:
   a. Is usually considered to be primary storage.
   b. Spins at 33 $1/3$ revolutions per minute.
   c. Can store a very large number of characters in a relatively small space.
   d. Costs about the same as a magnetic tape cassette.
8. A modern large scale computer can perform about how many multiplications in one second?
   a. 100 to 1,000
   b. 10,000 to 100,000
   c. 1,000,000 to 10,000,000
   d. 100,000,000 to 1,000,000,000
9. The Jacquard loom is:
   a. A bird found in southern France and northern Italy.
   b. A weaving machine that uses punched cards to specify the raising and lowering of threads.

c. The first computer-controlled loom, built in the early 1950s.
d. A machine for automatically producing mathematics tables.

10. Herman Hollerith is best known for:
    a. Serving as president of IBM from 1902 to 1942.
    b. Building the first mechanical computer, called an analytical engine.
    c. Developing punched cards and data processing ideas used to process the U. S. Census data for 1890.
    d. Building the first relay computer in the 1930s.

11. The typical modern computer:
    a. Contains more than 10,000 vacuum tubes.
    b. Uses small magnetic cores for its secondary storage.
    c. Uses magnetic tape and/or disk for primary storage.
    d. Makes use of large scale integrated circuitry, called chips.

12. John von Neumann is well known for his contribution to:
    a. Design of computers.
    b. Help in developing game theory.
    c. Mathematics.
    d. All of the above.

13. If a computer program is quite short (less than 20 statements long) we can conclude:
    a. It will take less than one second to run on a computer.
    b. It is bug-free, since it is so short.
    c. It is not long enough to perform a useful task.
    d. None of the above.

14. Information to be processed by a computer is called:
    a. Records.
    b. Data.
    c. Intelligence.
    d. Files

15. Most errors blamed on computers used in business are actually due to:
    a. Hardware problems.
    b. Programming errors.
    c. Data preparation and data entry errors.
    d. None of the above.

16. Key to tape and key to disk refer to:
    a. The locks found on most tape and disk cabinets.
    b. Indexes used in retrieving information from tape or disk.
    c. Data entry devices.
    d. Output devices.
17. A flowchart is best defined as:
    a. A chart or record showing weekly flow of programs through a computer.
    b. A diagram showing the flow of electricity through a computer memory.
    c. A two-dimensional picture, using boxes and connectors, showing a step-by-step set of directions.
    d. A computer-produced analysis of the steps needed to solve a problem.
18. BASIC is an example of:
    a. A language all computers understand.
    b. A language designed to be read and used by both people and computers.
    c. A natural language.
    d. A programming language most often used in business applications.
19. If a mail delivery robot working in an office building finds an obstacle in its path, it is most apt to:
    a. Blow a fuse.
    b. Signal for help.
    c. Remove the obstacle.
    d. Climb over the obstacle.
20. A thermostat is an example of:
    a. A microcomputer.
    b. An information retrieval machine.
    c. A process control device.
    d. Artificial intelligence.
21. A walking, talking robot is most likely to be found:
    a. Working in a modern factory.
    b. Teaching in a school or university.
    c. Working as a computer operator.
    d. In a science fiction movie.
22. Computer applications for information retrieval include:
    a. Supermarket checkout systems using UPC.
    b. Airline reservation systems.

c. Computerized search of medical literature.
d. All of the above.

23. Currently the people making the most use of full text searching are:
    a. Airline reservation clerks.
    b. Police.
    c. Lawyers.
    d. English teachers.

24. Data processing is:
    a. Any use of computers that produces data.
    b. The collection, storage, and processing of data to produce needed reports.
    c. The retrieval of data stored in a computerized data bank.
    d. All applications of computers outside the field of business.

25. A computer program for a mathematical model is called:
    a. A computer simulation.
    b. Artificial intelligence.
    c. A large scale integrated circuit.
    d. Computer graphics.

26. Word processing refers to the use of computers to:
    a. Alphabetize the words going into a new dictionary.
    b. Help automate a typewriter.
    c. Solve word puzzles.
    d. Try out various letter combinations in order to create new words.

27. Most things computers do:
    a. Can be done in other ways.
    b. Can only be done by computers.
    c. Can be done more cheaply if larger computers are used.
    d. Can be done more reliably by hand.

28. At the current time computers are:
    a. Able to take over most functions of a first grade teacher.
    b. Handling much of the administrative work in secondary schools.
    c. Becoming commonplace in medical education.
    d. Too expensive to use in schools.

29. With respect to computers and automation, it is correct to say:
    a. Computers are primarily responsible for our current levels of unemployment.
    b. Computers have helped wipe out many jobs but have helped create other jobs.
    c. That each computer displaces 15-20 workers.
    d. Computers are creating about two million jobs a year.

30. Large scale or national data banks are not a threat to privacy because:
    a. Truth cannot hurt people.
    b. They are prohibited by law.
    c. They are used only for our benefit.
    d. None of the above is correct.

31. The first step in using a computer library program to solve a problem is to:
    a. Gather all data and facts relevant to the problem.
    b. Find a computer library program designed to solve the problem.
    c. Understand the problem.
    d. Write the necessary program and place it in a computer library.

32. Computers can play checkers and chess fairly well, but currently they are not very good at:
    a. Language translation.
    b. Medical diagnostic work.
    c. Teaching students simple arithmetic.
    d. Storing and retrieving large amounts of information.

33. In solving a problem, a computer:
    a. Thinks much like a person.
    b. First has to understand the problem.
    c. Follows a program, written by people.
    d. Usually recalls the answer from memory.

34. Which of the following abbreviations is not commonly used in computer science?
    a. CRT
    b. IBM
    c. UPC
    d. ECT

35. A computer program:
    a. Lists instructions to the computer operator.
    b. Is about the same thing as a flowchart.
    c. Is a television program about computers.
    d. Contains exact instructions for each step needed to solve a certain type of problem.

GLOSSARY

Access Time. The time required to gain access to needed data. A modern computer can access data from storage very quickly. Examples: from primary storage—less than 1 microsecond; magnetic disk—25-100 milliseconds; magnetic tape—50 milliseconds to several minutes.

Algorithm. A finite, step-by-step set of directions designed to solve a particular type of problem. Computers can sometimes carry out some of these steps. Examples are long division, square roots, or others that are studied in mathematics courses.

Analog Computer. A kind of computer that uses continuously varying quantities such as length, voltage, current, or weight to represent and solve problems. Analog computers are often used by scientists and engineers.

Arithmetic and Logic Unit (ALU). The central processing unit of a computer consists of two main parts. One part, called the control unit, figures out the meaning of the instructions in a program. The other part, called the arithmetic and logic unit, actually carries out the instructions. The ALU is much like a superspeed calculator.

Artificial Intelligence. The branch of computer science that develops computer systems to do intelligent-like tasks, such as game playing, question answering, language translation, and carrying on a conversation.

Binary. Consisting of two parts or two things. Binary arithmetic uses two symbols, ∅ and 1, to represent numbers. Most computer storage devices are designed to store binary digits, and the computer circuitry is designed to manipulate information coded in a binary form.

Binary Digit. One of the symbols ∅ or 1. Often abbreviated as bit. A sequence of binary digits can be used as a code for letters or numbers to be processed by a computer.

BASIC. **B**eginners **A**ll-purpose **S**ymbolic **I**nstruction **C**ode. The most widely used computer programming language in elementary and secondary schools. It was designed to be easy for students to use in solving problems.

Bug. An error—usually in a procedure or in a computer program. However, it can also refer to a hardware error.

Business Data Processing (BDP). The use of computers to process the types of data needed in running a business. See also **Data Processing**.

Calculator. A device for carrying out calculations. A pocket calculator is not a computer, but can do arithmetic. A calculator has provisions for inputting data, specifying the operations to be performed and outputting answers.

Cathode Ray Tube (CRT). The type of vacuum tube used as the picture tube in a TV set, and as the display screen in many computer terminals.

Central Processing Unit (CPU). This is the heart of a computer system. It consists of the control unit and the arithmetic and logic unit. In a microprocessor the CPU may be built into a single chip.

Character. A letter, digit, punctuation mark, or other symbol. An electronic digital computer is designed for the input, storage, manipulation, and output of such characters.

Chip. Integrated circuits and large scale integrated circuits are manufactured on a small "piece" of silicon. Such a circuit can contain many thousands of transistors and related electronic components, and is often called a chip.

Computer. A device that can input, store, manipulate, and output data. It can automatically follow a program (a detailed step-by-step set of directions). Two major categories are **Analog Computers** and **Digital Computers.**

Computer Graphics. The use of computers to deal with picture-type information. A computer terminal with a graphics display screen is a common input/output device for computer graphics. Pen-and-ink plotting devices are also comonly used.

Core. A very common form of primary memory or storage. It is an iron, donut-shaped ring, about 1 mm in diameter. Sometimes the primary memory of a computer is called **Core Memory** even though it does not contain cores, but instead is made up of transistorized devices (chips).

COBOL. A widely used programming language called **C**ommon **B**usiness **O**riented **L**anguage. It was developed in 1960 to meet the specific needs of the Business Data Processing field.

Data. Facts, recorded measurements, and other information. In the computer field, the word data usually refers to information to be processed by a computer.

Data Bank. A collection of data. Often this term refers to a computerized collection of information about people, and occurs in a discussion of privacy and security.

Data Processing. The processing of (raw) data to produce information and reports and/or to solve problems. If it is business data, the process is called **Business Data Processing**.

Debug. To remove the bugs (errors) from a procedure or computer program. Key ideas include detecting the presence of a bug and locating its precise cause.

Digital Computer. A kind of computer that uses characters (digits, letters, punctuation marks) to represent data and programs. A digital computer can be thought of as an automated character manipulation machine.

Disk. A storage device consisting of a flat circular rotating surface coated with magnetic iron oxide. It is usually used as *secondary* storage and looks like a phonograph record. Access time to a disk is about 25 to 100 milliseconds.

Electromechanical. An electrically powered device with many mechanical, moving parts. Some early calculators were powered by a hand crank. Replacing the hand crank with an electric motor made them electromechanical calculators.

Electronic Funds Transfer (EFT). The transfer of money from one account into another via electronic technology. For example, after computer terminals read a buyer's credit card, money is transferred from the person's bank account to the store's bank account.

ENIAC. The **E**lectric **N**umerical **I**ntegrator **A**nd **C**alculator which was the first general purpose electronic digital computer. It was built at the University of Pennsylvania and became operational in December 1945.

File. A collection of related records treated as a unit. For example, detailed information about one student might constitute a record, and all records for one school might constitute a file.

Flowchart. A diagram consisting of various shaped boxes and connectors to display a procedure. A flowchart gives a two dimensional picture of the steps of a procedure.

Full Text Searching. The retrieval of certain information by searching the full text of an article or book stored in a computer's secondary memory. The computer finds the information by looking for desired words or phrases.

Graphics. See **Computer Graphics.**

Hardware. The physical machinery of a computer system. It includes the central processing unit, primary storage, secondary storage, input devices, and output devices.

Information Retrieval. A branch of computer science having to do with the storage and retrieval of information. Generally it is concerned with large files of information (data banks).

Instruction. A step of a computer program, which a computer is designed to carry out. Examples of instructions could be to add two numbers or to access data stored on a disk.

Integrated Circuit. See **Chip.**

Keyboard Terminal. A computer input and output device with a typewriter-like keyboard and a display mechanism (paper or CRT).

Keypunch. A device used by a person to punch holes (representing characters of information) into a card, so the card can be read by a card reader.

Large Scale Integrated Circuit (LSI). A circuit consisting of many hundreds or thousands of transistors and other electrical components, and manufactured as a single unit. See **Chip.**

Line Printer. A computer output device that seems to print an entire line at a time. Speeds of 300-1800 lines per minute are common, and line lengths can be 80 to 132 characters long. Thus, such printers may be hundreds of times as fast as a human typist.

Loop. A sequence of instructions that causes an activity to be performed repeatedly. The repetition may continue indefinitely (an indefinite loop) or until some predetermined condition is satisfied (a conditional, or finite loop).

Machine Language. The instruction set a computer is designed to be able to "understand." Instructions in machine language can be stored in a computer's memory, interpreted by its control unit, and executed by its arithmetic and logic unit.

Magnetic Core. See **Core.**

Magnetic Ink Character Recognition (MICR). The use of ink containing magnetic particles so that printed characters can be read by a machine. The most common use is on bank checks.

Magnetic Disk. See **Disk**.

Magnetic Tape. The magnetic tape used for secondary storage on a computer system. It is much like that used on a home tape recorder, although it often is of higher quality. Recording densities of 800, 1600, or 6250 characters per inch are common. Thus a large reel of tape can store many millions of characters of information.

Mainframe. A computer system's hardware consists of a mainframe and peripherals. The mainframe includes the central processing unit and primary storage.

Mathematical Model. A model employing mathematical formulas. An example is $E = mc^2$ which relates energy, mass, and the speed of light. See **Modeling**.

Memory. A computer's storage device(s). Most computers have a primary memory with very fast access which is relatively small, and secondary storage which can contain a large number of characters of information, but has slower access time. See also **Core, Magnetic Tape,** and **Disk**.

Microprocessor. A one-chip central processing unit.

Microsecond. One-millionth of a second. A modern computer can access information in its primary memory, or add two numbers, in less than one microsecond.

Millisecond. One-thousandth of a second. Useful in discussing speeds of computer peripherals such as input/output devices and secondary storage. The access time for a disk might be 25 to 100 milliseconds.

Modeling. The process of accurately describing or representing certain parts of a system. A key aspect of science, used to state what will happen under a particular set of circumstances. See **Simulation**.

Nanosecond. One-billionth of a second. A very fast modern computer can access main memory or add two numbers in a few nanoseconds. In one nanosecond light (in a vacuum) travels a little less than one foot, or electricity in a wire travels about nine inches. Thus, very fast computers must be physically small.

Optical Character Recognition. The machine reading of typewritten or handwritten characters. The typewritten or careful handwritten materials are now commonly read by computers, but computer reading of general human handwriting is still a research problem.

Optical Mark Reader. The machine reading of mark sense cards or sheets. Often used for scoring tests or recording grades.

PASCAL. A modern programming language, developed for computer science instruction.

Peripheral Equipment. A computer system consists of a mainframe and peripheral equipment. Peripherals include secondary storage, card reader, line printer, and other input/output devices.

Primary Storage. The fast-access part of a computer's memory system. It operates at a speed comparable to the arithmetic and logic unit. It is generally much smaller in storage capacity than the secondary storage part of the memory system.

Procedure. A finite step-by-step set of directions that can be mechanically interpreted and carried out by some agent. Computer science is concerned with situations in which the agent is a computer, or perhaps a human assisted by a calculator, a computer, or a robot-like device.

Process Control. The use of machinery (perhaps computers) to control a process. It involves the input of data that represents measurements on the process, processing of the data to decide upon appropriate action, and automatically taking the action.

Program. A detailed step-by-step set of directions telling a computer how to perform a procedure. It may be written in a high level language such as BASIC or COBOL, or in a particular computer's machine language. The words program and procedure are sometimes used interchangeably.

Programmable Calculator. A calculator-like device with certain computer-like features. A programmable digital calculator can store a program (a sequence of key strokes) in its primary memory or in secondary storage, and can execute a stored program. Such machines are well suited to certain science, engineering, and business computations.

Punch Card. A card that can be punched with holes that can stand for letters, numbers or symbols. The holes represent information that can be used to control machines. A keypunch machine is used to punch the character codes into a card.

Relay Computer. A computer making use of electromagnetic switches to carry out computations. It was built in the 1930's and early 1940's before the much faster electronic computer was developed.

Robot. A machine or device that works automatically. It usually carries out limited tasks but it can be made more versatile when a computer is used in it.

Record. A group of related pieces of computerized information. For example, a student's transcript might be one record, and the collection of all transcripts for a school might be one file.

Remote Terminal. A computer input/output device that is located some distance from the computer. It is generally in another room or building or even another city.

Secondary Storage. The slow access part of a computer's memory system. It may consist of magnetic disks, magnetic tape devices, bubble memory, and/or charge-coupled devices.

Simulation. Carrying out the steps or computations of a model in order to determine what will happen in a given set of circumstances. When done by use of a computer it is called computer simulation. See **Modeling**.

Software. Computer programs. Examples include programs written by students as well as much larger programs such as a BASIC or COBOL translator.

Terminal. An input or output device. See **Keyboard Terminal**.

Timesharing. A method of computer usage, or type of computer system where many people use the computer at the same time. The computer system shares its resources among its users through different terminals.

Translator. A computer program that translates instructions written in a language such as BASIC or COBOL into a form the computer hardware understands.

Universal Product Code (UPC). The dark colored parallel lines on a grocery item (containing the company number and the item number of the product). It can be read by a laser reading device and input to a computer.

Word Processing. The use of computers to help automate a typewriter. Materials are typed and stored in a computer memory where they can be changed. Final copy is then typed out very quickly by the computer.

ANSWERS TO TEST QUESTIONS

Chapter 2	Chapter 3	Chapter 4	Chapter 5	Chapter 6
1. F	1. F	1. T	1. T	1. T
2. T	2. T	2. T	2. T	2. F
3. F	3. T	3. T	3. F	3. F
4. T	4. F	4. F	4. F	4. T
5. F	5. F	5. F	5. T	5. T
6. T	6. T	6. T	6. F	6. F
7. F	7. T	7. T	7. T	7. F
8. T	8. T	8. F	8. F	8. T
9. F	9. T	9. T	9. F	9. T
10. T	10. F	10. F	10. F	10. F

Chapter 7	Chapter 8	Final Exam			
1. F	1. F	1. b	11. d	21. d	31. c
2. T	2. T	2. d	12. d	22. d	32. a
3. T	3. F	3. a	13. d	23. c	33. c
4. F	4. F	4. b	14. b	24. b	34. d
5. T	5. T	5. a	15. c	25. a	35. d
6. F	6. F	6. a	16. c	26. b	
7. T	7. T	7. c	17. c	27. a	
8. T	8. T	8. c	18. b	28. c	
9. T	9. F	9. b	19. b	29. b	
10. F	10. T	10. c	20. c	30. d	

About the Authors...

DR. DAVID MOURSUND is a well-known computer science educator who has written four other books on computers and computing. He has written numerous papers on computer education and is probably best known for his work with elementary and high school teachers. This is his fourth book.

KAREN BILLINGS, along with DAVID MOURSUND, has helped pioneer the use of computers in U.S. schools. A former junior high school teacher and editor of The Oregon Mathematics Teacher, she is currently pursuing her doctorate at the Teachers College at Columbia University. She is Director of the Microcomputer Resource Center at Teachers College. This is her second book.

MORE HELPFUL WORDS FOR YOU

Computers for Everybody, 2nd Edition
Jerry Willis and Merl Miller

In a clear, understandable way, this new edition explains how a computer can be used in your home, office or at school. If you're anxious to buy a computer, use one, or just want to find out about them, read this book first.
ISBN 0-88056-094-0 $7.95

The Tenderfoot's Guide to Word Processing
Barbara Chirlian

This informative book introduces word processing and its many uses. Described in great detail is a specific word processing program called Executive Assistant.
ISBN 0-918398-58-4 $10.95

Nailing Jelly to a Tree
Jerry Willis and William Danley, Jr.

This is a book about software. The emphasis is on learning to use the thousands of available programs that have already been written, and adapting them to your machine.
ISBN 0-918398-42-8 $15.95

Small Business Computer Primer
Robert McCaleb
Delta Group, Inc.

Here is a solid overview of computer selection in layman's business language. The book contains unbiased information which tells you how to successfully evaluate and select a small computer system.
ISBN 0-88056-067-3 $14.95

 dilithium Press, P.O. Box E, Beaverton, OR 97075
Call our toll-free number — 800-547-1842 — to charge your order on VISA or M/C.

Send to: dilithium Press, P.O. Box E, Beaverton, OR 97075

Please send me the book(s) I have checked. I understand that if I'm not fully satisfied, I can return the book(s) within 10 days for full and prompt refund.

____ Computers for Everybody, 2nd Ed.   ____ A Tenderfoot's Guide to Word Processing
____ Nailing Jelly to a Tree   ____ Small Business Computer Primer

☐ Check enclosed $_____   ☐ Please charge my
    Payable to dilithium Press   ☐ VISA ☐ Mastercharge
☐ Send me your catalog of books.   #_____ Exp. Date_____

                              Signature _____

Name _____
Address _____
City, State, Zip _____